THEMATIC UNIT

Amphibians and Reptiles

Written by Janna Reed

Teacher Created Materials, Inc.
6421 Industry Way
Westminster, CA 92683
www.teachercreated.com

©*2000 Teacher Created Materials, Inc.*

Made in U.S.A.

ISBN-1-57690-378-8

Illustrator
Chandler Sinnott

Contributing Editor
Janet A. Hale, M.S. Ed.

Cover Art by
Agi Palinay

Table of Contents

Introduction

Amphibians and Reptiles is a captivating unit featuring fascinating amphibians and reptiles from around the world. At the core of this literature-based unit are two selections: a fiction story, *Ferret in the Bedroom, Lizards in the Fridge* and a nonfiction resource book, *The World's Most Spectacular Reptiles and Amphibians*. Activities have been suggested to enhance the use of both selections, as well as connections to language arts, science, social studies, math, life skills, and art. Opportunities for higher-level thinking are also provided for strengthening critical and analytical skills, logical and deductive-reasoning skills, and problem-solving abilities. The unit's culminating activities allow for synthesizing the knowledge gained as well as serving as an assessment of student knowledge.

This thematic unit includes the following:

- ☐ **literature selections**—with related lessons which cross the curriculum

- ☐ **planning ideas**—suggested for sequencing your lesson plans

- ☐ **writing ideas**—which extend across the curriculum

- ☐ **bulletin-board ideas**—for creating interactive bulletin boards

- ☐ **curriculum connections**—including language arts, science, social studies, math, life skills, and art

- ☐ **group projects**—to encourage cooperative learning

- ☐ **culminating activities**—designed to synthesize student learning via assessment-oriented experiences

- ☐ **bibliography**—listing additional fiction and nonfiction titles, CD-ROMs, and videos

---

To keep this valuable resource intact so that it can be used year after year, you may wish to punch holes in the pages and store them in a three-ring binder.

Introduction (cont.)

Why a Balanced Approach?

The strength of a balanced language approach is that it encourages students to use all modes of communication—reading, writing, listening, illustrating, and doing. Communication skills are interconnected and integrated into lessons that emphasize the whole of language. Implicit to this approach is the knowledge that every whole—including individual words—is composed of parts, and directed study of those parts can help a student master the whole. Experience and research tell us that regular attention to phonics, other word attack skills, spelling, etc., helps develop reading mastery. Students should be regularly encouraged to read, write, spell, speak, and listen in response to a literature experience. In these ways, language skills grow rapidly, stimulated by direct practice, involvement, and interest in the topic at hand.

Why Thematic Planning?

A useful tool for implementing an integrated and balanced language program is thematic planning. By choosing a theme with correlative literature selections, a teacher can plan activities throughout the day that lead to a cohesive in-depth study of the topic. Both teachers and students are then freed from a day that is broken into unrelated segments of isolated drill and practice. Students will also be practicing and applying their skills within a meaningful context. Consequently, they will learn and retain more educational information.

Why Cooperative Learning?

Besides academic skills and content, students need to learn social skills. No longer can this area of development be taken for granted. Students must learn to work cooperatively in order to function well in modern society. Group activities should be a regular part of school life, and teachers should consciously include social objectives as well as academic objectives in their planning. For example, a group working together to write a report may need to select a leader, writer, researcher(s), and illustrator(s). The teacher should make clear to the students the qualities of good leader-follower group interactions, just as he or she would state and monitor the academic goals of a project.

Why Journals?

Each day students should have the opportunity to write in a journal. They may respond to a book or an event in history, write about a personal experience, or answer a general "question of the day" posed by the teacher. The cumulative journal provides an excellent means of documenting the students' writing progress.

Ferret in the Bedroom, Lizards in the Fridge

By Bill Wallace

Summary

Liz Robbins lives in a zoo—at least that's what her friends think. Liz's dad is a zoologist who likes to be surrounded by his work—literally! Because of the animal menagerie, Liz's friends are afraid to visit her home. She finally decides the animals must go. When the animals depart, Liz realizes that she really did enjoy having them be a part of her life.

The outline below is a suggested plan. Adapt them as needed to suit your classroom needs.

Sample Plan

Lesson 1

- Discuss the differences between amphibians and reptiles (page 6, Setting the Stage #2).
- Read Chapters 1–2. After discussing the chapters, assign Liz and Lizard Probability (page 11).
- Have your students create Gecko Links (page 65).

Lesson 2

- Review the events of Chapters 1-2 and read Chapters 3–6.
- Assign Turtle Trails (page 12).
- Create Turtle-Shell Patterns (page 52).
- Challenge the students to memorize the turtle poem (page 28); reward them if they do!

Lesson 3

- Read Chapters 7–13.
- Read and discuss herpetile as pets (page 6, #4).
- Discuss the concept of designer snakes (page 6, #6).
- Create Illusions in Locomotion (page 39).
- Try out some Snake Tricks (page 66).

Lesson 4

- Review the main story events thus far; read Chapters 14–16.
- Discuss the main characters' personality traits using Who am I? (page 8).
- Complete Cause and Effect (page 9).
- Assign the Book Review (page 10).
- Extend logical and critical thinking with Can You Solve the Problem? (page 13).

Overview of Activities

Setting the Stage

1. Create a Bill Wallace Author Center (Bibliography, page 78). Discuss the different types of stories in the range of his writings. Encourage general-interest reading as well by creating A Reading Metamorphosis bulletin-board display (page 73) near the author-center area.

2. The term *herpetology* or *herpetofauna* means the study of amphibians and reptiles. Ask the students to share experiences they have had with herpetofauna. Encourage them to describe whether the experiences were funny, scary, or made them feel brave. Also discuss the differences between the two categories:

   Amphibians are often mistaken for reptiles. The term amphibian means double lifestyle. They are scaleless creatures that, with a few exceptions, live part of their lives in the water and part on land. There are about 4,000 kinds of amphibians. They are also a part of the Vertebrate class.

   Reptiles are dry, scaly-skinned animals that breathe by means of lungs. There are 6,500 reptile species and they make up one of the classes of Vertebrates, animals with backbones.

3. Create interest in the world of herpetofauna by making Gecko Links (page 65). Let the students decorate the classroom or their desks with a string of linked geckos.

Enjoying the Book

1. Read Chapters 1–6 of *Ferret in the Bedroom, Lizards in the Fridge*. Discuss the care and feeding chores mentioned in these chapters. Use Liz's feelings about feeding the lizards to lead into the Liz and Lizard Probability activity (page 11).

2. Discuss the effect of Liz forgetting to put the board back in the doorway. Investigate the possibilities of the turtles' wanderings with Turtle Trails (page 12). Have the students look at examples of different turtles' shell designs. Point out the fact that shell patterns differ depending on the species and in what geographical regions the turtles are found. Assign Turtle-Shell Patterns (page 52).

3. After reading Chapters 7–13, discuss what is happening to Liz. Ask the students if they sympathize with her. Do they have any suggestions for Liz?

4. Read and discuss Herpetile Pets (page 59). Ask the students if they think the Robbins family follows the guidelines outlined on this page. Allow them to create pamphlets to advertise the proper care and handling of herpetiles.

5. Finish reading the book. After analyzing the characters' personalities (page 8), discuss the causes and effects of the story's events. Were any of the effects due to certain personality traits?

6. Have the students list popular brands of clothing, shoes, or sunglasses. Discuss the reason designer items are higher priced (high demand, better quality products). Besides designer wear, there are also designer snakes. These snakes are not killed for their skin, rather they are purchased as pets because of their unique skin patterns. Use Designer Snakes (page 60) to discuss the economics of supply and demand.

6

Overview of Activities *(cont.)*

Extending the Book

1. Encourage logical and critical thinking by utilizing open-response problems, such as: What would have happened if Liz had never gotten rid of the animals? First ask your students to work on these problems individually. After they have written their responses, place them in small discussion groups to present their individual viewpoints. Have the groups share responses with the entire class. Record the shared statements on the chalkboard or chart paper. Let the class decide if the views are similar enough to be in agreement or if they are distinctly different. Help them understand that scientists often have varied viewpoints.

2. Have the students complete a Book Review (page 10). Invite them to also use this form after reading other Bill Wallace books (Bibliography, page 78).

3. Many cultures have used turtle shells and Rattlesnake rattlers as musical instruments. Have your students make one or both of these herpetile instruments.

Turtle-Shell Rattles

Use two paper bowls to act as a turtle's shell. Draw and paint designs to represent the carapace (upper shell) pattern on the bowl and the plastron (lower shell) pattern on the other. Place a small handful of dried beans in one of the bowls. Place a thick ring of glue along the edge of that bowl. Place the second bowl on top of the first, matching the edges. Gently press the bowls' rims together. Allow the glue to dry thoroughly.

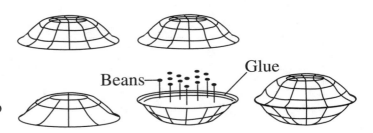

Turtle-Shell Rattle

Snake Tambourine

Using a hammer and nail, punch a small hole in the center of twenty metal bottle caps. Alternating the punched caps with small wooden or plastic beads, thread a wire through the caps and beads to form a snake. Twist the ends of the wire together, making the "snake circle" just loose enough for it to rattle. If desired, paint the snake's bottle caps to simulate a snake's color-warning pattern. For example, if the caps are painted using a black, yellow, and red band pattern, it will represent a venomous Coral snake's coloring. There are sayings that go with the color-warning snake patterns: If red touches yellow—kill that fellow! If red touches black—it's safe, venom lack.

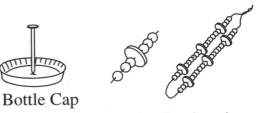

Bottle Cap   Snake Tambourine

Who Am I?

Which characters in the story do the word groups describe? Write the correct character's name in each box after reading the clues.

1. • is an organizer
   • anxious to work on campaign
   • doesn't give up easily
   • likes to make plans

4. • prissy
   • oozy-sweet voice
   • fake, gushy giggle
   • snooty smile

2. • frightens easily
   • afraid of animals
   • screams a lot
   • biggest gossip in school

5. • easily embarrassed
   • not very confident
   • didn't give up
   • has animal friends

3. • good at making dumb looks
   • slugs people
   • calls people names
   • enjoys embarrassing people
   • curls lips into a nasty smile

6. • handsome smile
   • concerned for feelings of others
   • considers animals friends

Name Box

Shane	Tina	Ted	Jo Donna	Liz	Sally

Cause and Effect

Match the cause with its effect.

Cause

_____ **1.** Mr. T felt the need to protect himself.

_____ **2.** Liz realized the animals were friends, too.

_____ **3.** A lizard got loose during Show-and-Tell.

_____ **4.** Tina screamed.

_____ **5.** Liz didn't take home her gym clothes for two weeks.

_____ **6.** Sally decided to help Jo Donna campaign instead of helping Liz.

_____ **7.** Liz forgot to put the board down in the bottom of the doorway.

_____ **8.** The girls wanted an ice cream snack.

_____ **9.** Sally tried to help Liz with her appearance.

_____ **10.** Shane liked animals.

_____ **11.** Daddy told Liz that Bessie does the best she can with what she's got.

_____ **12.** Liz blamed the animals for her not having friends.

_____ **13.** Liz decided to be bright, happy, and full of life, just like Fred.

Effect

A. Josh and Mr. T leave the kitchen area.

B. Mr. T ate Liz's sock.

C. Jo Donna called her Miss Piggy.

D. Everyone stared at Liz's red face and hair.

E. Shane and Liz became friends.

F. Liz's name became Lizard.

G. By afternoon, people began to respond and the disastrous morning turned into an okay day.

H. Mr. T wet on the white blouse.

I. Liz decided not to feel sorry for herself.

J. All of the animals were gone, except for Fred and Ivan.

K. A lizard was found wrapped in tin foil.

L. Liz got her animal friends back and gained a new friend as well.

M. He released a foul odor from his musk glands.

Book Review

Title

_____

Author

_____

Problem

_____

_____

_____

Plot *(Describe how the situation, or problem, was developed in the story.)*

_____

_____

_____

_____

_____

_____

Conclusion *(Explain how the problem was solved.)*

_____

_____

_____

Rating *(Was the author effective in getting the reader involved? Why or why not?)*

_____

_____

Liz and Lizard Probability

There are 3,800 species of lizards. Liz's dad has 15 species of lizards on their porch: 9 kinds of chameleons, 3 kinds of geckos, 1 kind of skink, and 2 kinds of iguanas.

One evening Dad was in the kitchen. He asked Liz to bring him a chameleon, a gecko, and a skink. When Liz went out to get the animals, she noticed the porch light had burned out. Liz could not see very well. What will she bring to her dad?

Use the following probability formula to answer the following questions:

$$\text{probability} = \frac{\text{\# of favorable outcomes}}{\text{\# of possible outcomes}}$$

1. What is the probability that Liz will catch a chameleon?_____ or _____

2. What is the probability that she will catch a gecko? _____ or _____

3. What is the probability that a skink will be caught? _____ or _____

4. What is the probability that one of the species she wants to catch will be caught the first time? _____

Probability can also be expressed as a percentage. Use the probability gauge to answer the following questions.

5. What is the percentage of probability that Liz will catch...

   a chameleon? _____

   a gecko?   _____

   a skink?   _____

6. Which lizard species is least likely to be caught?

_____Why?_____

7. Which species is most likely to be caught?

_____Why?_____

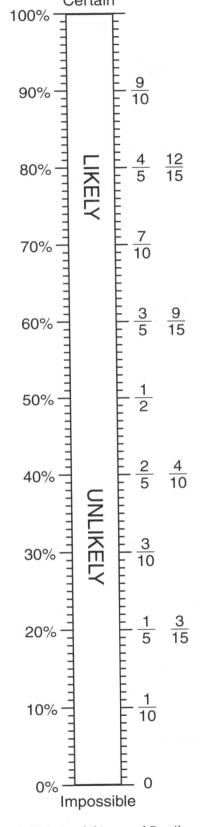

Turtle Trails

Liz doesn't like feeding lizards because she doesn't like crickets. She made a deal with Mom by telling her, "You feed the lizards and I'll mop the floor." The turtle trouble began when Liz forgot to put the board back up in the doorway after mopping the floor and the turtles go out.

Suppose there were 40 turtles. Using the tree diagram below, mathematically answer the following questions.

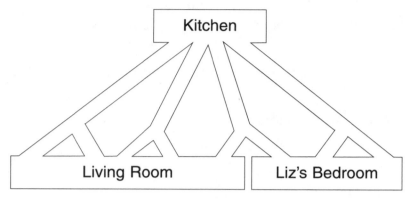

How many turtles would most likely end up in the living room? _____

How many turtles would most likely end up in Liz's bedroom? _____

Mathematically explain your answers. _____

_____

_____

Using the following floor plan, how many turtles would most likely be found in the living room? _____

How many would mostly likely be found in her parent's bedroom? _____

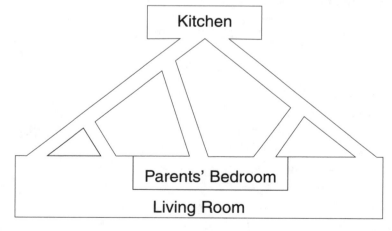

Mathematically explain your answer. _____

_____

_____

Can You Solve the Problem?

1. Liz's friend, Shane, and his parents have left town for a few weeks. Shane has asked Liz to take care of his pet snakes. Liz knows that Shane likes to regularly measure them and record their growth. Liz is frustrated with this task! None of the snakes will be still and stretch out.

   List two possible methods Liz could use to measure the snakes.

   _____

   _____

   _____

   _____

   _____

2. Liz's dad does not keep a Gila Monster or a Mexican Beaded lizard on the porch because these two lizards have venom glands. These reptiles are kept at a local university zoology department. Liz has been thinking: *These reptiles only eat eggs. If eggs are their natural diet, then why do these animals need venom?*

   Give Liz a possible explanation.

   _____

   _____

   _____

   _____

   _____

3. Sally had an idea that she shared with Liz. She thinks Liz should move the turtles out onto the porch where the lizards are kept.

   Explain to Sally why this might, or might not, be a good idea.

   _____

   _____

   _____

   _____

   _____

The World's Most Spectacular Reptiles and Amphibians

By William Lamar

Summary

Reptiles and amphibians are exotic and fascinating creatures. They are also often misunderstood. This book provides useful information designed to create awareness of the benefits these animals provide for humans. In addition, the photographs will mesmerize your students with their vibrant colors and detail.

The outline below is a suggested plan. Adapt them as needed to suit your classroom needs.

Sample Plan

Lesson 1

Acquaint your students with the herpetofauna in this book by showing them the photographs.

- Begin the Classification activity (page 34).
- Provide deductive-reasoning experiences via Ectotherms or Endotherms? (page 36).
- Discuss the categories for endangerment, then assign the Endangerment Chart and Map (pages 46–48).
- Have the students use multiple resources to complete Defense Mechanisms (pages 42–43).
- Assign Species Populations (pages 55–56).

Lesson 2

Today's focus is on reptiles. Re-look at the reptilian photographs.

- Complete Let Me Out! (page 27).
- Construct Serpentine Food Miniwheels (page 20).
- Create inside-outside snakes (page 16, Enjoying the Book, #3).
- Conduct Flying Dragon experiments (page 37).

Lesson 3

Today's focus is on lizards. Re-look at the lizard photographs.

- Assign Stick out Your Tongue (page 26).
- Discover the effects of Chromatophores (page 44).
- Read Dara's Tuatara (page 28).
- Have your students complete What is a Tuatara? (page 53).
- Create Gharial Designs (page 62).

Lesson 4

Today's focus is on frogs and toads. Re-look at the frog and toad photographs.

- Discover Amphibious Genetics (page 41).
- Make Female Surinam Toads (page 18).
- Create Pigmentation Color Wheels (page 64).
- Have students analyze The Call of the Wild (page 57).

Lesson 5

Today's focus is a general herpetofauna review. Re-look at your favorite photographs.

- Construct herpetofauna Eyes and Eyelids models (pages 24–25).
- Discover Unusual Uses for herpetofauna (pages 50–51).
- Buy some Special Snacks (page 61).
- Assign Try to be Distinctive (page 32).
- For extra-credit, assign These are Laws? (page 16, Extending the Book, #4).
- Conduct the Turtle Simulation (page 71).

Overview of Activities

Setting the Stage

1. If you have not already done so, create a Reptile and Amphibian Resource Nook complete with pictures, books, posters, videos, pamphlets, and, if available, computers with CD-ROMs (Ask an Expert, page 77; Bibliography, page 78).

2. Review the differences between amphibians and reptiles (page 6, Setting the Stage, #2). Complete Amphibians (page 17) as a total group, and then in small groups, challenge them to create reptilian Venn diagrams choosing some of their favorite reptiles.

3. Ask the students if they have ever visited any reptile and/or amphibian exhibits. Ask them to share their experiences about how the animals were displayed. Discuss whether or not they think the animals' living areas were similar to, or not similar to, the animals' natural habitats.

4. Discuss any prior knowledge the students have concerning the environmental effects on amphibians and reptiles. If the students are unresponsive, pose these questions:

   - *Are you aware that highways that bisect habitats cause amphibians deaths?* (The animals have to go back to the ponds or lakes to spawn.)

   - *Do you know that habitats are reduced due to housing and business developments?* (When land areas are scraped away, the animals die due to suffocation or displacement.)

   - *Can you think of a way in which habitat destruction affects food chains?* (If one of the food chain links is broken, the food chain's natural flow is totally stopped or disrupted to such a point that other food chain cycles will be affected.)

5. Reproduce, on tagboard, one Vocabulary Pocket (page 29) per student. Using scissors, cut out the pockets on the bold outer lines as well as slit open the dashed lines, using a razor blade or sharp knife. Provide each student with a prepared pocket and reproduced Vocabulary Ts sheets (pages 30–31). To create a stand-up display, have them fold their Vocabulary Pockets in half on the fold line. Next have them cut out the Ts and slide them categorically into the cut slits. The Vocabulary-Pocket Ts can be used as a reinforcement tool to aid in correct spelling and word meanings. (A blank T is also provided for you or the students to add a word or words of choice to the vocabulary-pocket display holder.)

Enjoying the Book

1. Introduce the students to the animal groups represented in the book by introducing the Classification project (page 34). After the students have researched and filled in the Classification Cards (page 35), have them cut out and tape the fill-in cards in the correct column of a prepared Families chart-paper display with these labeled column headings: Snakes, Lizards, Turtles, Tortoises, Crocodiles, Alligators, Frogs, Salamanders, Caecilians.

2. After finishing Sample Plan: Lesson 1 (page 14), your students should be ready to delve further into the characteristics and behaviors of herpetofauna. Construct Flying Dragons (page 37) and permit the students to conduct gliding experiments.

Overview of Activities *(cont.)*

Enjoying the Book *(cont.)*

3. Ask your students to create a snake's inside-and-outside body features by first completing pages 22–23. Then have them cut out both snakes' outlines. Using one of the two cut shapes as a pattern, have them place the snake shape onto a piece of plain, white paper and trace the outline of the snake's body; remove the snake shape and cut out the third snake shape. Using uncooked, old-fashioned oats, glue down individual oat scales onto the white shape to form the snake's scales. Be certain the students refer to the Scales sheet (page 21) for correct placement. Once completed, layer the three paper snake shapes—scales, skeleton, and internal organs—and staple them near the snake's head area; display.

4. Once you are certain that the students understand the characteristics of amphibians and reptiles, they can create fictional stories in which animals' physical characteristics are mixed-up. After the stories are written and illustrated, allow a sharing time so that they can read one another's stories.

5. Looking at the photographs in the book, can the students identify any reptiles they may have seen in movies? Have them name those movies. Then, if possible, allow them to create multimedia presentations featuring a selected herpetofauna, using a slide-show format.

6. Our world is full of strange creatures. Have the class conduct research on the Surinam Toad and then complete the activity found on page 18.

Extending the Book

1. The eyes have it! Some amphibians and reptiles have unusual eyelids. Discover their movements by completing Eyes and Eyelids (pages 24–25).

2. Introduce Try to be Distinctive (page 32). Have the students write a magazine article, focusing on the most important elements needed for this style of writing.

3. Assign the Fear! activity (page 33). Guide the students towards brainstorming how to create a persuasive piece and what information needs to be included.

4. Have the students conduct research pertaining to the These Are Laws? activity sheet (page 49). To do this successfully, they will need to use State Statute reference books. These are available at most local and/or university libraries. Encourage the students to write their state legislators about any laws that are obsolete or current that pertain to issues concerning reptiles and/or amphibians.

5. Encourage letter writing by having your students write to a variety of amphibian and reptile organizations (see Ask an Expert, page 77).

Amphibians

Amphibians are animals that live on land and/or in water at some time during their developmental stages and adulthood. Decide how the following characteristics should be placed on the Venn diagram.

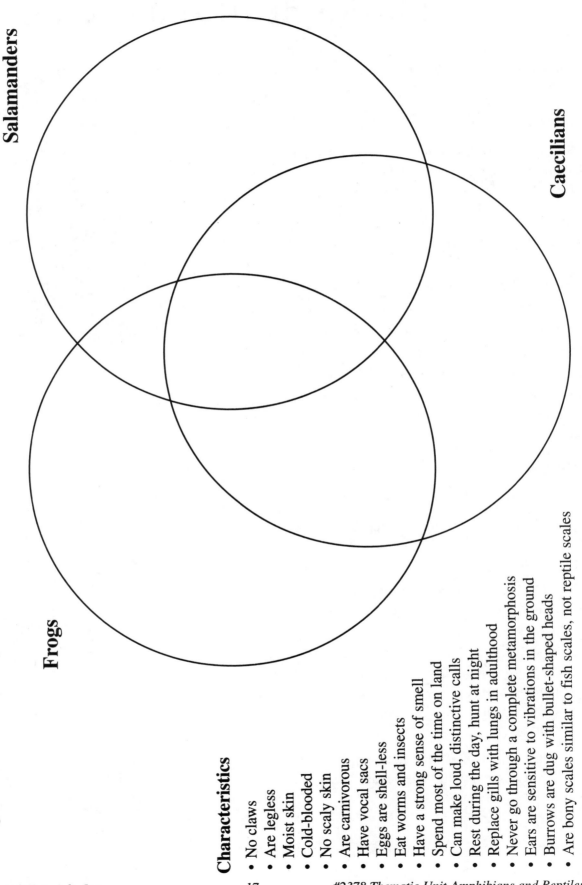

Salamanders

Caecilians

Frogs

Characteristics

- No claws
- Are legless
- Moist skin
- Cold-blooded
- No scaly skin
- Are carnivorous
- Have vocal sacs
- Eggs are shell-less
- Eat worms and insects
- Have a strong sense of smell
- Spend most of the time on land
- Can make loud, distinctive calls
- Rest during the day, hunt at night
- Replace gills with lungs in adulthood
- Never go through a complete metamorphosis
- Ears are sensitive to vibrations in the ground
- Burrows are dug with bullet-shaped heads
- Are bony scales similar to fish scales, not reptile scales

Female Surinam Toads

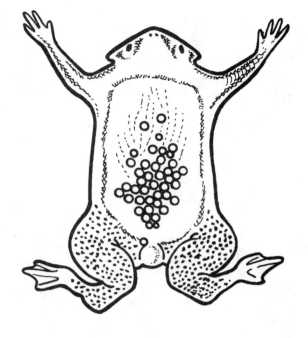

Surinam toads are one of the strangest amphibians. They are found in the Orinoco and Amazon Basins of South America. They have flat heads and pig-like eyes. Being completely aquatic, Surinam toads only occasionally leave their pond or stream habitat.

Surinam toads do not progress through the normal stages of amphibian growth. The male presses his fertilized eggs onto the back of the female. Soon the eggs sink into pits located in her back skin. The female carries these fertilized eggs in her birthing pits until fully formed froglets emerge and swim away.

Materials (per student)

- Surinam Female Toad Pattern (page 19)
- tan 9" x 12" (23 cm x 30 cm) construction paper
- blue 9" x 12" (23 cm x 30 cm) construction paper
- brown markers, colored pencils, or crayons
- a razor blade
- scissors
- glue

Preparations

1. Reproduce the Surinam Female Toad pattern onto the tan construction paper.

2. Using the razor blade, carefully slit the dashed lines.

Directions

1. Color the female Surinam and her babies a mix of light and dark browns; cut out the toad and her babies.

2. On the backside of the toad, carefully place a ring of glue around its perimeter. Glue the body onto the blue sheet of construction paper. (Caution: Be certain no glue has gotten into any of the slit pit areas.)

3. Place the babies into the female's birthing pits (slit circles) with their heads sticking out.

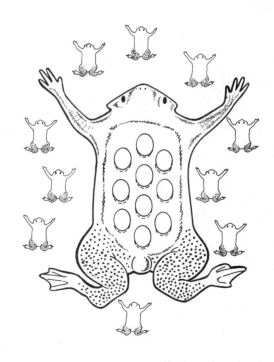

18

Female Surinam Toad Pattern

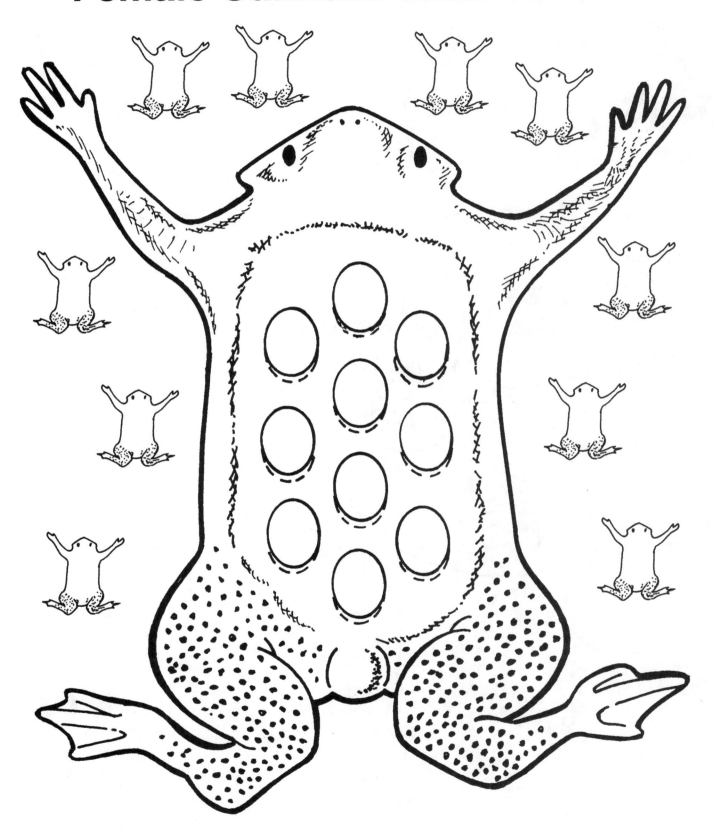

Serpentine Food Miniwheel

Cut out the three wheels. Stack the three wheels: A (top), B (middle), and C (bottom). Push a brad fastener through the three wheels; open brad fastener. Turn the wheels until the type of snake and its preferred food is displayed through the viewing window by matching the symbols.

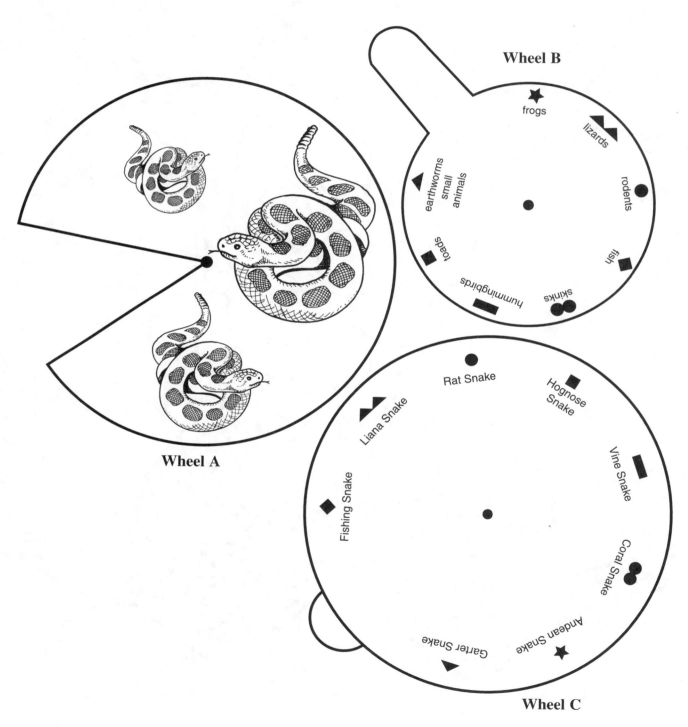

Wheel A

Wheel B

Wheel C

Scales

Snakes and lizards have three basic types of scales.

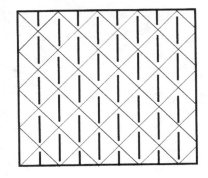

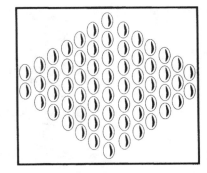

Smooth   **Keels** (Ridges)   **Granular** (Bead-like)

Snake and lizard scales are made of *keratin*. Human fingernails are also made of keratin. Reptilian scales are actually covered by a thin layer of skin. The outer layer of skin is shed several times a year depending on the species, its growth patterns and health, and even weather conditions. Most snakes and lizards eat their shed skin. This behavior is called *dermatophagy*.

There is a method for counting snake scales. The diagram demonstrates the process.

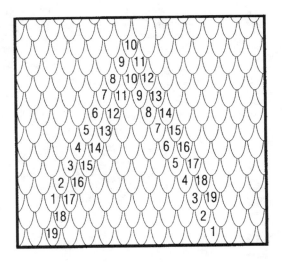

A Rattlesnake's rattle is also made of keratin. An old wives' tale is told that the look of its rattle can tell you how old the Rattlesnake is. This is not true. An individual rattle section is added every time a Rattlesnake sheds its outer skin.

Inside, Outside 1

Each segment of a snake's backbone is called a vertebra. There are two ribs attached to each vertebra. These series of vertebra and ribs protect the inner organs and help support its long body. A pair of muscles is attached to each rib section to aid in the snake's movements.

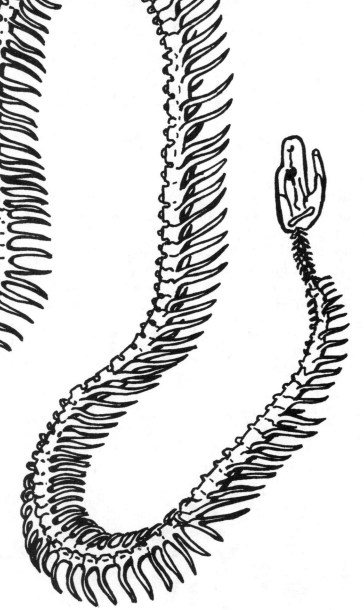

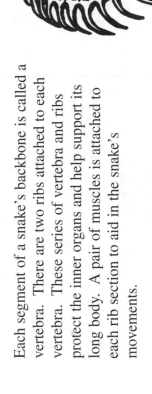

Look closely at this snake skeleton.

Approximately how many sets of muscles does this snake have? _____

Inside, Outside 2

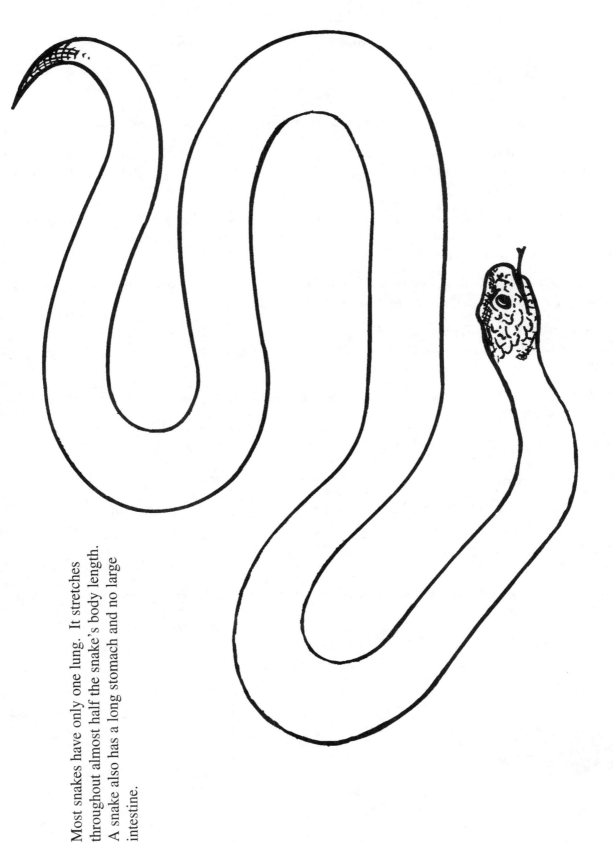

Most snakes have only one lung. It stretches throughout almost half the snake's body length. A snake also has a long stomach and no large intestine.

Using a reference book, draw in these internal organs: heart, lung, stomach, and small intestine. Draw any other additional organs mentioned or shown in your reference materials.

Eyes and Eyelids

Round

Vertical-Elliptic

Horizontal-Elliptic

Most **lizards** and **skinks** have *round* pupils and moveable (closing) eyelids. The Burrowing skink has a unique clear eyelid "window" in its lower lid. When it closes its eyes it can still see through the bottom lid, yet keep out dirt and debris.

Nocturnal **geckos** have *vertical-elliptic* pupils, while diurnal (daytime feeder) geckos have *round* pupils. Most geckos do not have moveable eyelids. Their eyes are always open. A transparent scale called a spectacle protects each eye.

Snakes' pupils are *round* or *vertical-elliptic*. They have no eyelids. They also have spectacles. The pupil shape of a snake's eye is not an indication of the presence of poison.

Most **frog** families have *horizontal-elliptic* pupils, the exceptions being the Burrowing and Spadefoot toad families, which have *vertical-elliptic* pupils. Frogs' bottom eyelids move upward and cover the entire pupil area.

Crocodilians have *vertical-elliptic* pupils with three moveable eyelids per eye: a semi-transparent lid, the upper lid, and the lower lid.

For an "eye-opening" experience, complete these two eye-action simulations.

Frog Eyelid Action

1. Cut out the Pupil and Eye squares. Cut out the Eye's center circle; discard circle.
2. Cut out the Eyelid's paddle shape.
3. Place the Eye square directly on top of the Pupil square. Tape the left, top, and right sides together.
4. Insert the Eyelid's flat end into the untaped opening. Slide the Eyelid upward to simulate a frog closing its eyelid.

Pupil

Eye

Eyelid

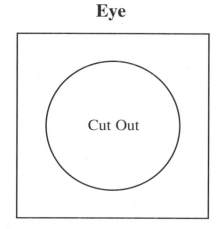

Cut Out

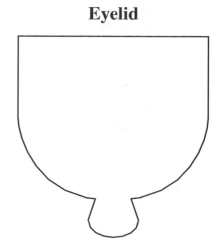

Crocodilian Three-way Eyelid Action

Directions

1. Cut out the five eye parts. Cut out the Semi-Transparent Lid's and Eye's center sections; discard cut-out sections.

2. Using a small piece of transparent plastic wrap, cover the Semi-Transparent Lid's open area; tape the wrap's edges to this section's frame.

3. Place the Semi-Transparent Lid on top of the Pupil's rectangle so that the pupil can be seen through the transparent wrap.

4. Place the Top and Bottom lids on top of the Semi-Transparent Lid.

5. Place the Eye rectangle directly on top of the layered Lid's rectangle. Tape the right side-edges only. Carefully manipulate the three lids to demonstrate a crocodile's eyelid's three-way movement (Semi-Transparent lid—Top lid—Bottom lid).

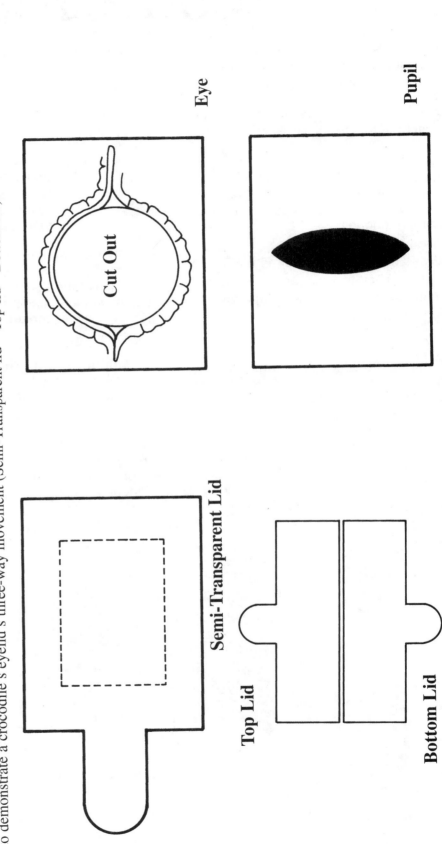

Eye

Pupil

Semi-Transparent Lid

Top Lid

Bottom Lid

Stick Out Your Tongue

In the Animal kingdom, tongues are not only used for eating, but also as a form of warning or protection. For example, the Australian Blue-tongued skink sticks out its bright-blue tongue and hisses loudly when it is threatened.

Read each tongue description. Then study the tongue shapes. Write the animal's name under its matching tongue shape.

Geckos bark, shriek, chirp, or cluck depending on their species. Geckos have wide, rounded tongues similar to human tongues.

Glass lizards are known as legless lizards. Their tongues are wide at the base and have an almost separate forked tongue at the tip.

Iguanas are vegetarians. Iguanas have a rounded tongue that is a little thicker and longer than a gecko's tongue.

Worm lizards live underground. They have no legs, eyes, or ear openings. Worm lizards have wide, slightly pointed tongues.

Skinks are diurnal (active during the day) and most species are insect-eaters. Skink tongues are longer and wider than most night-feeding lizard tongues, with a very small, forked tip.

Monitor lizards are carnivorous (meat-eaters). They have an extremely long, forked tongue.

Terrestrial lizards are quick on their feet. They have long tongues, with an equally long, forked-tongue section.

1._____

2._____

3._____

4._____

5._____

6._____

7._____

26

Let Me Out!

Egg-hatching animals need help to get out of their shells. A baby snake has a tiny, sharp tooth at the front of its mouth called an egg tooth, which is used to slice open its shell. A hatching crocodile or turtle has a hard bump at the end of its nose called an egg caruncle that is used to help break out of its shell. Conduct research to discover the differences between these three reptile's eggshells.

	Snake	Crocodile	Turtle
Reptile	egg tooth	egg caruncle	egg caruncle
Description of the Egg			
Drawing of the Egg			
Interesting Egg Facts			

Poetry

Dara's Tuatara

I know a girl named Dara,
Who has a Tuatara.
With a grin on his little face,
She takes him 'round from
place to place.
Like a tiny dinosaur,
He has not two, but legs a-four.
His back is lined with many
spikes,
And the thing that he really
likes,
Is riding Dara's racing bike.
If I could be just like Dara,
And have my very own Tuatara,
I'd put a helmet on that tyke,
And ride him around on my
touring bike!

Don't Be Fooled!

Reptiles! Reptiles!
Turtles, snakes, crocodiles,
Tuataras, and lizards, too,
Scales green and bellies blue.
Spiky spines and plated backs,
Legless crawlers making tracks,
Swiveling eyes and sticky toes,
Which are friends and which are
foes?
Laying eggs and shedding skin,
Wearing shells for living in,
Cold-blooded, forked tongue,
Changing colors in the sun.
Though they lurk in many places,
Don't be fooled by friendly faces.
Know your friends among reptiles,
For even foes wear flashy smiles!

There was a Little Turtle

There was a little turtle and he lived in a box,
He swam in the puddles and he climbed on the rocks.
He snapped at a mosquito, he snapped at a flea,
He snapped at a minnow, and he snapped at me!
He caught the mosquito, he caught the flea,
He caught the minnow—but he couldn't catch me!

Vocabulary Pockets

See #5 on page 15 for directions for this activity.

Amphibian and Reptilian Words

Fold

Reptilian Words

Amphibian Words

Vocabulary Ts

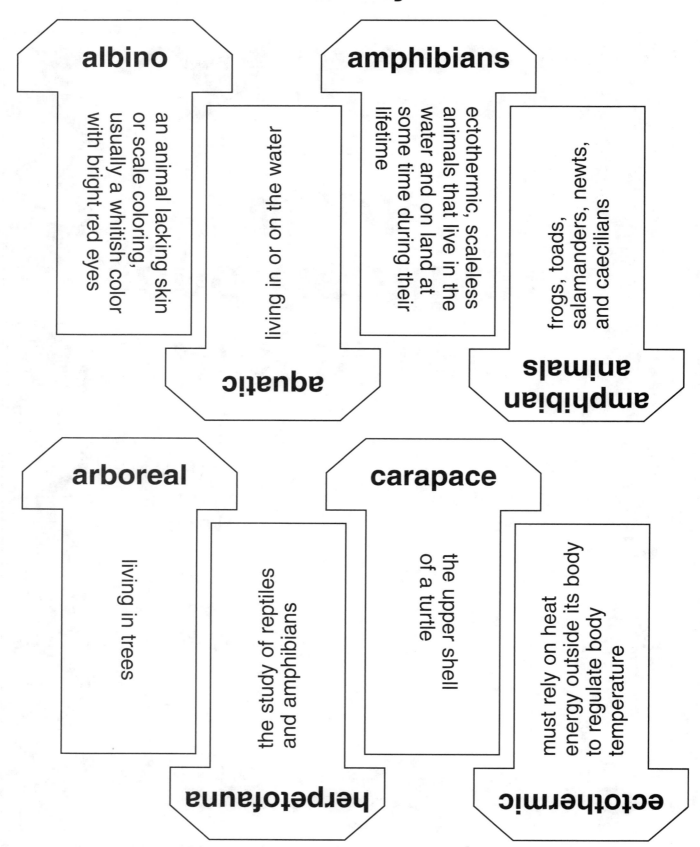

albino

an animal lacking skin or scale coloring, usually a whitish color with bright red eyes

aquatic

living in or on the water

amphibians

ectothermic, scaleless animals that live in the water and on land at some time during their lifetime

amphibian animals

frogs, toads, salamanders, newts, and caecilians

arboreal

living in trees

herpetofauna

the study of reptiles and amphibians

carapace

the upper shell of a turtle

ectothermic

must rely on heat energy outside its body to regulate body temperature

Vocabulary Ts *(cont.)*

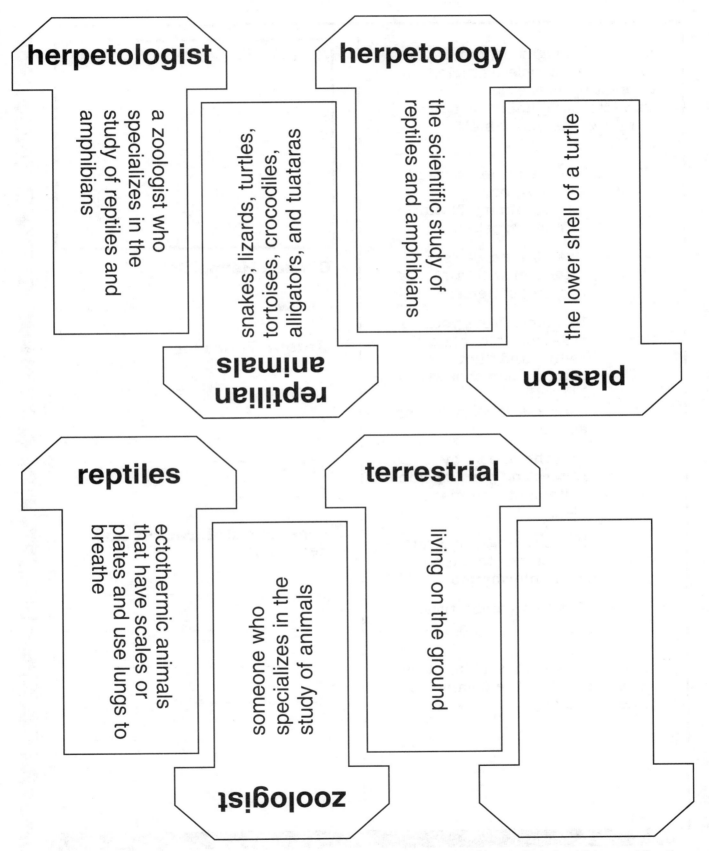

herpetologist

a zoologist who specializes in the study of reptiles and amphibians

snakes, lizards, turtles, tortoises, crocodiles, alligators, and tuataras

reptilian animals

herpetology

the scientific study of reptiles and amphibians

the lower shell of a turtle

plastron

reptiles

ectothermic animals that have scales or plates and use lungs to breathe

someone who specializes in the study of animals

zoologist

terrestrial

living on the ground

Try to be Distinctive

A student magazine wants you to write an article featuring an interesting herpetile characteristic, habit, or action. Here are the magazine's guidelines:

- ☐ 1. Choose an interesting, unusual, or extraordinary feature of one herpetile.

- ☐ 2. Grab the reader's attention with a strong opening statement.

- ☐ 3. Use facts from your research to explain the "why" and "how" behind your chosen herpetile's characteristic, habit, or action.

- ☐ 4. End the article by reiterating your opening statement and main idea.

- ☐ 5. Use drawings, diagrams, or pictures to support your information.

- ☐ 6. Create a catchy title.

As you write your article, place a check mark in the completed guideline boxes.

Chosen Herpetile

_____

Unique Features

_____

_____

_____

_____

Research References and Resources

_____

_____

_____

_____

_____

Fear!

In the reptilian world there are no poisonous turtles or crocodilians and only two venomous lizards: the *Gila Monster* and the *Mexican Beaded lizard.* There are more venomous snake species than any other reptile group, but most snakes are not poisonous.

Less than 10% of all snakes have venom that is capable of harming people. Snakes seem to cause more panic and fear in humans than any other reptile. Interestingly, the snakes people fear most may not be the most deadly. For example, *Sea snakes*, which have one of the most toxic venoms, are usually very docile and rarely bite people. *Coral snakes* also have highly toxic venom, but few people have been killed from their bite because they are generally shy and gentle creatures. The *Cottonmouth* and *Copperhead snakes*, whose venom is also highly toxic, inject far less venom than their maximum permits; therefore, if someone is bitten, they usually survive. While this is true, snakes with a much lower toxicity level can still be quite deadly. For example, the *Gaboon Viper*, *King Cobra*, and *Rattlesnake* have a low poison (toxicity) level, but inject tremendous amounts of venom, thus killing their victims.

Amphibians, frogs, salamanders, and *caecilians* also use toxins to protect themselves. Some of these toxins leave only an unpleasant taste in the attacker's mouth, while others are deadly. A toad has special glands located on each side of its neck that secrete "white poison." If a predator catches the toad in its mouth, the poison irritates its mouth and throat, causing nausea, an irregular heartbeat, and sometimes, death. One of the most powerful animal venoms is from the red and black *Arrow Poison frog.* South American natives collect this frog's poison by holding it over a fire. The heat causes the toxic fluid to form in droplets on the frog's skin. The extracted toxin is then placed on the tips of their hunting arrows. One ounce of this frog's poison is enough to kill 100,000 animals!

Can venom be useful? *Russell's Viper* venom is used to clot the blood and stop bleeding in hemophiliacs (people with bleeding disorders). Some substances in toad poison have the same effect as the drug Digitalis, which is given to heart patients to affect their heartbeats. Kokoi is a neurotoxin found in frogs that is used to help some people with nerve impulse disorders. Some secretions from frogs and toads have also been found to be effective antibiotics.

Writing Time

Using the above information, write a persuasive essay convincing the reader that knowledge of venomous animals and the use of caution may lessen their fear. You may choose to write your persuasive piece in a pamphlet form for extra points—and possible distribution!

Classification

Scientists classify, or group, animals according to similar characteristics. Classes are divided into Orders, which are then divided into Families. Most of the time, there are many Species in a given Family.

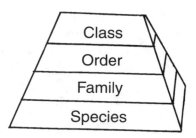

Class: **The Reptilie Class is divided as follows:**

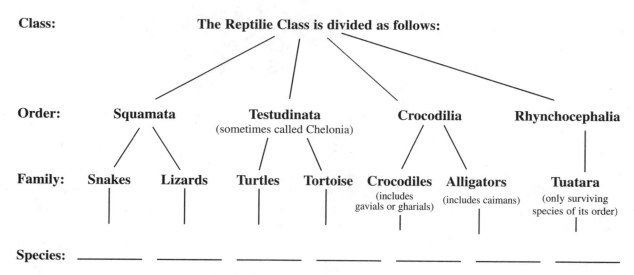

(Fill in the species names of your choice.)

The Amphibian Class is divided as follows:

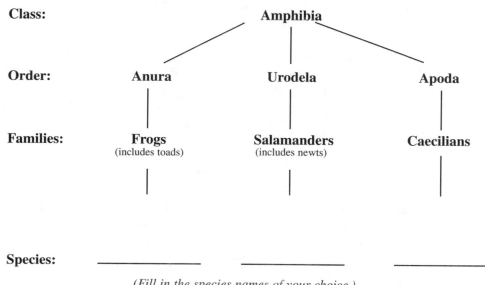

(Fill in the species names of your choice.)

Classification Cards

Choose one reptilian and one amphibian species. Using available resources, fill out a card for each of your chosen species.

Class _____ Order _____

Family _____ Species _____

Habitat _____

Diet _____

Arboreal? _____ Terrestrial? _____

Aquatic? _____ Vulnerable? _____

Threatened? _____ Endangered? _____

Unusual Habits or Characteristics

_____

_____

_____

_____

Draw an illustration, including correct coloration.

Class _____ Order _____

Family _____ Species _____

Habitat _____

Diet _____

Arboreal? _____ Terrestrial? _____

Aquatic? _____ Vulnerable? _____

Threatened? _____ Endangered? __

Unusual Habits or Characteristics

_____

_____

_____

_____

Draw an illustration, including correct coloration.

Ectotherms or Endotherms?

The graphs below display the body temperatures of two different animals. The temperatures were recorded on the same day, at the same times, and the animals remained in their (respective) same places.

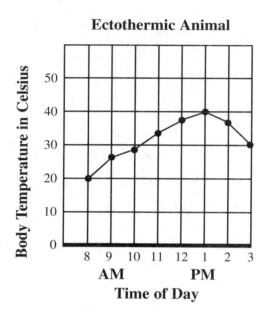

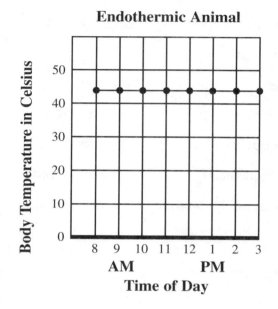

Using the graph information provided, create a definition for ectothermic and endothermic animals.

_____

_____

_____

_____

Draw and label a possible animal for each type.

Ectothermic

Endothermic

Flying Dragons

Flying Dragons, or Dracos, are found in southeastern Asia and the East Indies. These lizards are arboreal (tree dwellers) except for when they descend to earth to lay eggs. To move from tree to tree, they expand folds of skin attached to their sides that serve as natural gliders. When at rest, these folds are pressed against their bodies and are barely noticeable.

Construct an experimental Flying Dragon. Begin by cutting out the reproduced-on-tagboard lizard's body and tail patterns (page 38). Glue the tail to the body as the tabs indicate. Cut out the reinforcement strips; set aside. Using tissue paper for the skin expansions, follow the directions below to conduct your experiments.

Directions

1. From the tissue paper, cut out two 4" x 7" (10 cm x 18 cm) sections.

2. Using the 7" (18 cm) edge of one section, make a ½" (1.3 cm)-wide fold; crease folded edge. Continue folding the tissue paper using a traditional fan-folding pattern until the entire width has been folded; repeat with the second section.

3. Glue one of the reinforcement strips to one of the 7" (18 cm) edges of the tissue paper; set aside. Repeat the process with the remaining tissue-paper section and reinforcement strip.

4. Tape the unreinforced 7" (18 cm)-side edge of the two fanned tissue-paper sections to the lizard's sides (as indicated on the pattern) using transparent tape.

You are now ready to test-fly your lizard! Record the results of your lizard's first three flights in the Experiment 1 section of the chart. After your first three test flights, carefully remove your lizard's tissue-paper "wings" and try other expansion sizes to discover which size allows your lizard to glide the farthest. (**Note:** You will need to use fresh sheets of tissue paper and new reinforcements for Experiments 2 and 3.)

Experiment	Length of Tissue Paper	Width of Tissue Paper	Depth of Folds	Gliding Distance		
				Trial 1	Trial 2	Trial 3
1	4"/10 cm	7"/18 cm	½"/1.3 cm	___"/___cm	___"/___cm	___"/___cm
2	___"/___cm	___"/___cm	___"/___cm	___"/___cm	___"/___cm	___"/___cm
3	___"/___cm	___"/___cm	___"/___cm	___"/___cm	___"/___cm	___"/___cm

Which measurements allowed for the greatest flying distance? _____

Why?_____

Flying-Dragon Pattern

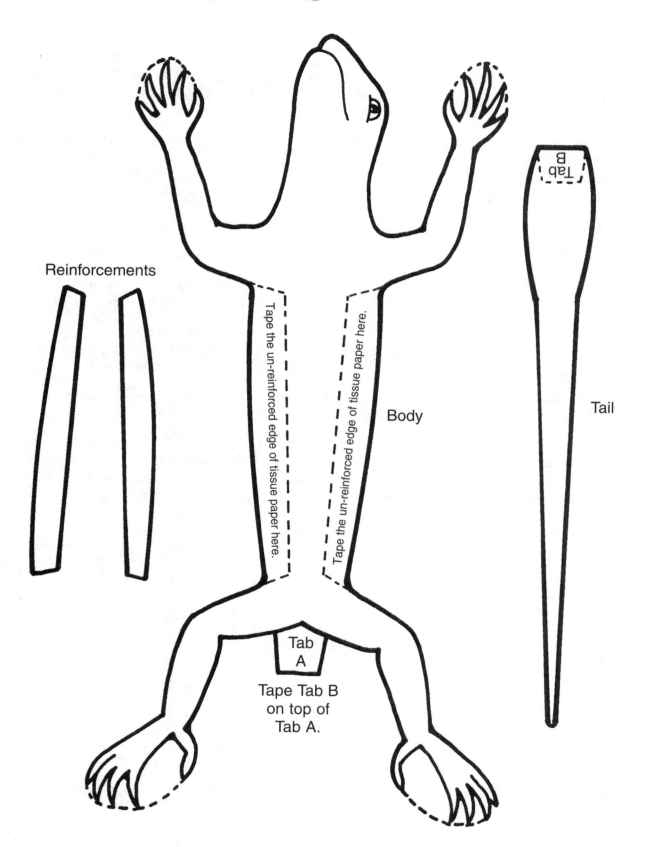

Reinforcements

Tape the un-reinforced edge of tissue paper here.

Tape the un-reinforced edge of tissue paper here.

Body

Tail

Tab B

Tab A

Tape Tab B on top of Tab A.

Illusions in Locomotion

Snakes have four main methods of locomotion:

Rectilinear   **Sidewinding**   **Concertina**   **Serpentine**

Big-bodied snakes, such as pythons, boas, and vipers, use a rectilinear motion. They press their large scales against the ground creating traction and moving their bodies in a straightforward motion.

Sidewinder snakes, such as the Namib Adder, literally lift portions of their bodies off the ground and thrust forward in a sideways motion. This form of movement keeps these snakes from falling down soft sand dunes and dusty trails.

Snakes that move with a concertina motion literally bunch themselves up and thrust themselves forward by quickly straightening their bodies.

Slender snakes, such as Rat snakes and Racers, move quickly by using a curving serpentine motion. This is accomplished when the sides of their bodies push against surface irregularities moving them forward. Visually create the serpentine movement by following these directions:

Materials

- one copy of Serpentine Locomotion Illusion (page 40)
- scissors
- one sheet of cardstock paper
- one sheet of black construction paper
- crayons or colored markers
- transparent tape
- sharp-pointed knife or razor blade (Adult supervision is required.)

Directions

1. Using the scissors, cut apart the two Locomotion Illusion sections; discard the cut-away paper.

2. Glue the straight-stripe section onto a piece of same-size cardstock; trim edges.

3. Choose two to three colors to decorate the white stripes. (**Note:** The illusion works best when there is a pattern to the colors.)

4. Cut a 1" x 7" (2.54 cm x 18 cm) pull-tab strip from the remaining cardstock. Tape the 1" (2.54 cm) pull-tab to the center back area of the striped section. (**Note:** The pull-tab should extend beyond one of the two *shorter* sides of the striped section.)

5. Using the sharp knife or razor blade (ask an adult to do this), cut out the white, curvy lines on the black section. (Be certain no white color remains after the lines have been cut out.)

6. Using the scissors, cut out a rectangle from the black construction paper that matches the curvy-lined box. Place the colored-stripe, tabbed section on top of the cut-out black construction paper rectangle.

7. Place the curvy-lined box on top of the placed striped section. Using the transparent tape, tape the top and side edges together.

8. Gently pull the tab downward to view the serpentine locomotion illusion.

Serpentine Locomotion Illusion

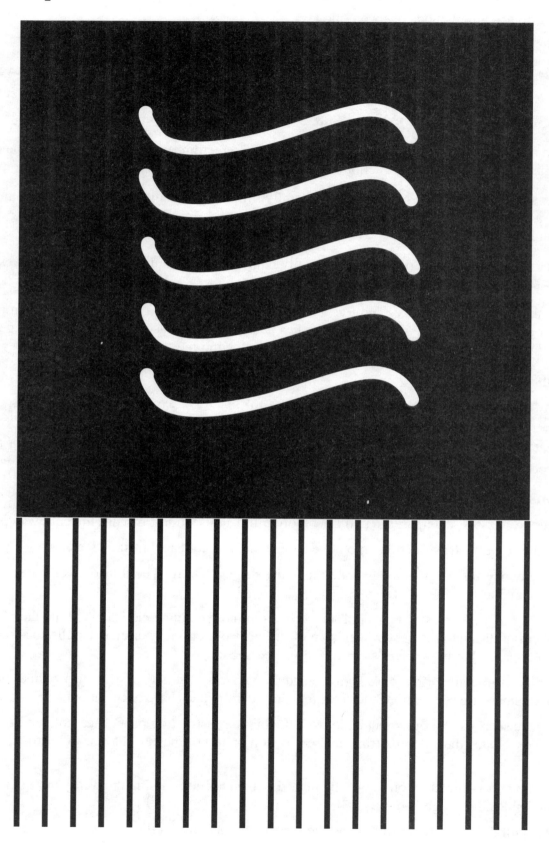

Amphibious Genetics

Every species has its own characteristics, or traits, such as coloring, shape, size, etc. Genes control how these traits are passed on to the offspring. Every trait has at least two genes—one from the male parent and one from the female parent. A gene that prevents another gene from being expressed is called a *dominant* gene. An unexpressed gene is called a *recessive* gene. An upper-case letter represents a dominant gene, while a lower-case letter represents a recessive gene.

Striped (S)   Mottled (s)

1. Which gene is dominant? _____ 2. Which gene is recessive? _____

First Generation

SS   ss
(striped)   (mottled)

Second Generation

Ss   Ss   Ss   Ss
(striped)   (striped)   (striped)   (striped)

Third Generation

SS   Ss   sS   ss
(striped)   (striped)   (striped)   (mottled)

3. How many generations did it take for a mottled patterned frog to occur? _____

4. What arrangements of genes can produce striped individuals? _____

5. What arrangements of genes can produce mottled individuals? _____

6. How does the presence of the dominant or recessive gene affect the color pattern of the frog?

_____

Reptile Defense Mechanisms

Research and discover the type of defenses used by the following herpetiles.

Reptiles	Defenses	Resources Used
American Box Turtle		
Australian Frill-necked Lizard		
Chameleon		
Garter Snake		
Gila Monster		
Hognose Snake		
Rinkhal Cobra		
Skink		

Amphibian Defense Mechanisms

Research and discover the type of defenses used by the following herpetiles.

Amphibians	Defenses	Resources Used
Amazon Harlequin Toad		
Axlotl		
Caecilian		
Giant Marine Toad		
Leopard Frog		
Marbled Salamander		
Plains Spadefoot Toad		
Red-spotted Newt		

Chromatophores

A feature of some herpetiles' skin is its ability to change color. Skin cells called *chromatophores* contain pigments and are responsible for the color change. Changes occur from fear, but also from fluctuations in the amount of light present, humidity, and air temperature. Warmer temperatures cause the chromatophore pigments to contract, which makes the dark-colored pigments harder to see. Therefore, the herpetile's skin becomes lighter. With cooler temperatures, the chromatophores usually spread out allowing more of the dark coloring to show. This causes the skin to appear darker. A few herpetiles can become a different color altogether. Two of these species are the Anole and the Chameleon. To view this amazing chromatophore phenomenon, follow the directions below.

Materials

- one copy of the Anole Grid (page 45), reproduced onto cardstock
- a green crayon or marker
- a brown crayon or marker
- scissors
- glue

Directions

1. Color Box A's Anole light green and its background dark green. Color Box B's Anole light brown and its background dark brown.

2. Cut away Box A and Box B. (Note: You will now have three sections: A, B, and C.)

3. Fold Box C on its dashed lines using an accordion-style-folding pattern; crease the fold lines. Re-open the folds and lay Box C as flat as possible on a desk or tabletop.

4. Carefully cut apart Box A along the dotted lines. (**Note:** Be sure you keep the nine cut strips in their correct sequential order.) From left to right, glue the green strips onto the Number 1-striped sections of the Box C accordion folds.

5. Carefully cut apart Box B along the dotted lines. (**Note:** Be sure you keep the nine cut strips in their correct sequential order.) From left to right, glue the brown strips onto the Number 2-striped sections of the Box C accordion folds.

6. After allowing the glue to dry, re-fold the accordion pleats. Unfold pleats slightly and place the Box C section in an up-right position. When viewing the folds from a left-side angle, a green Anole will be seen. When viewing the folds at eye level from a right-side angle, the Anole's chromatophores will have changed to brown.

Anole Grid

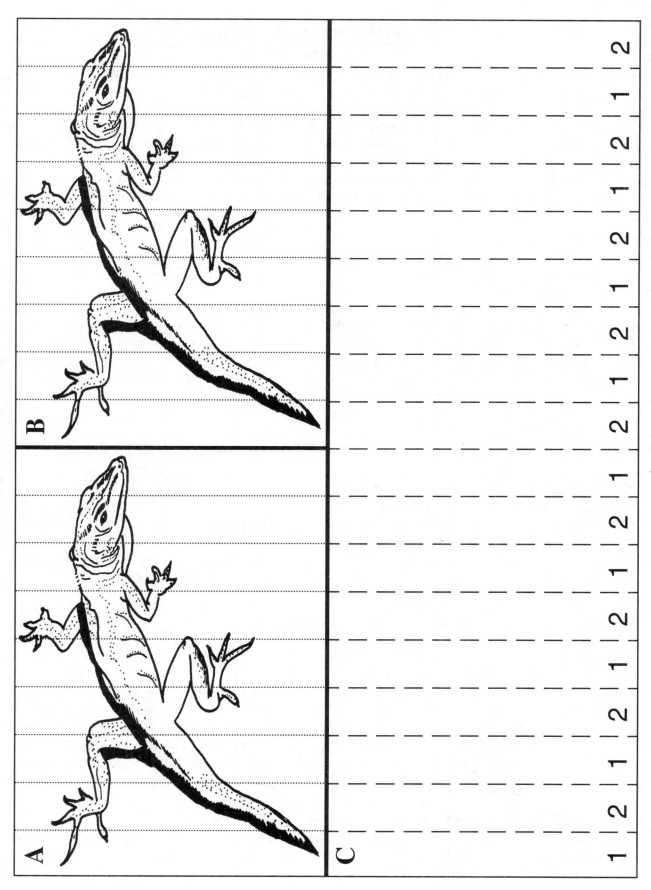

Endangerment

The North American species featured below are in the IUCN (International Union for the Conservation of Nature and Natural Resources) *Red List of Threatened Animals.*

List the herpetofauna name-and-location information found in each descriptive paragraph below on the Endangerment Chart. Determine into which endangerment category each species should be placed (vulnerable, endangered, rare, or extinct) and fill in the appropriate column. Record your endangerment-status reasons. Analyze your recorded data and draw conclusions as to what kind of actions should be taken to improve the chances of survival. List your suggestions in the last column.

Kemp's Ridley is the smallest known sea turtle. It is found in the Atlantic Ocean. Its numbers have been drastically reduced due to fishing nets and egg loss by animals and humans.

The **Florida Gopher Tortoise** is located in the Southeastern United States. It is moving towards a low population due to the destruction of its habitat by business growth and wild fires.

The **Axolotl** is found in Lake Xochimilco, near Mexico City. Its population may soon be affected by the introduction of a non-native fish that feeds on its eggs and larvae.

The **Vegas Valley Leopard Frog** has not been sighted since 1942. At that time is existed in Las Vegas, Nevada, but the development of this city has led to the total destruction of its habitat.

The **St. Croix Ground Lizard's** favorite habitat is in sandy areas along the coast of St. Croix in the Virgin Islands. Extremely low populations have occurred due to the construction of retaining walls along the coastline which have restricted its habitat.

The **California Black Legless Lizards'** habitat is decreasing due to an increased human population. They are at risk because no protective measures have been taken.

The **Eastern Indigo Snake** is one of the largest harmless snakes of North America. It can be found in Georgia, South Carolina, Alabama, and Florida. The greatest danger to this species is the high demand for the sale of its beautiful skin to collectors, commercial dealers, and breeders.

Endangerment Chart

Herpetofauna Name	Location	Endangerment Status	Reason for Status	Suggested Actions

Endangerment Categories

Vulnerable (V)

Species that are currently considered satisfactory but may soon be considered endangered if factors are not improved that threaten their habitats.

Endangered (E)

Species that are in danger of extinction due to low populations or greatly reduced habitats.

Rare (R)

Species found in very limited habitats with low populations.

Extinct (E)

No species has been identified in the wild in the last 50 years.

Endangerment Map

Label the habitat areas of the threatened herpetofauna species located in the name box.

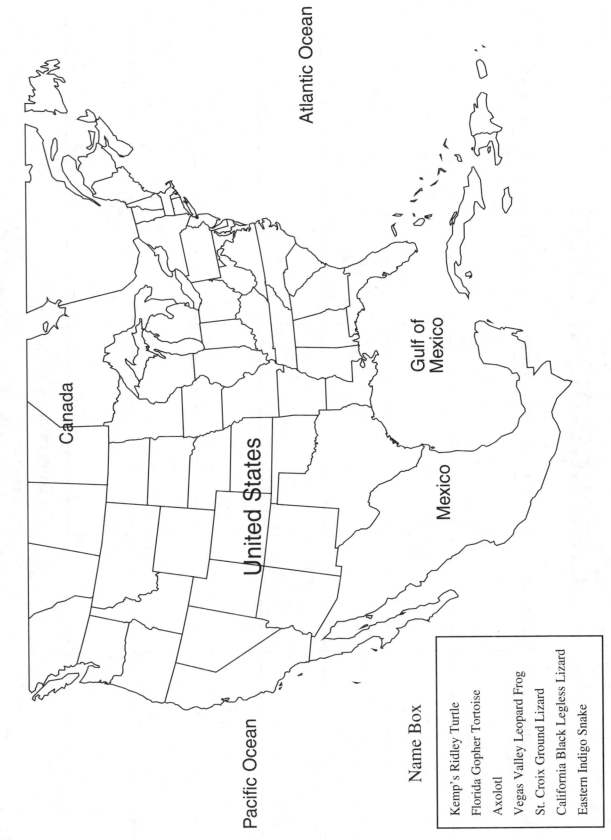

Atlantic Ocean

Canada

Pacific Ocean

United States

Gulf of Mexico

Mexico

Name Box

Kemp's Ridley Turtle
Florida Gopher Tortoise
Axolotl
Vegas Valley Leopard Frog
St. Croix Ground Lizard
California Black Legless Lizard
Eastern Indigo Snake

These are Laws?

Many reptile and amphibian laws or ordinances have been passed throughout the United States. At the time they were created, these regulations made perfect sense. Today, they seem strange indeed. Here are some examples:

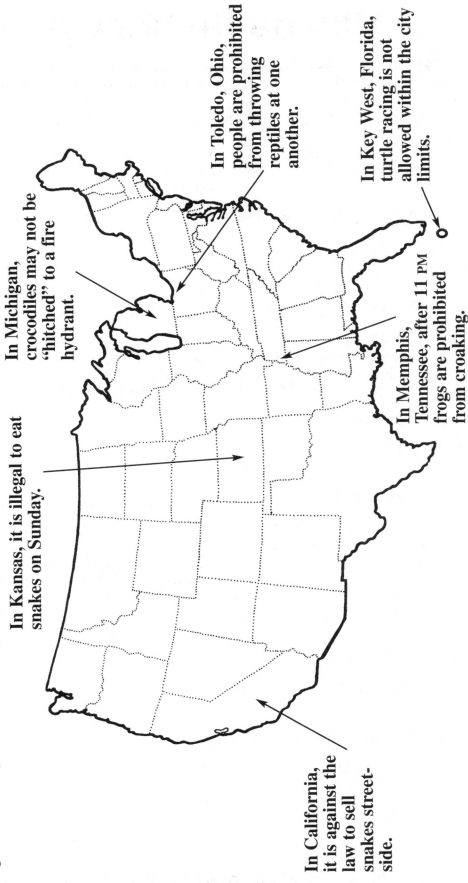

In Michigan, crocodiles may not be "hitched" to a fire hydrant.

In Kansas, it is illegal to eat snakes on Sunday.

In Toledo, Ohio, people are prohibited from throwing reptiles at one another.

In Key West, Florida, turtle racing is not allowed within the city limits.

In Memphis, Tennessee, after 11 PM frogs are prohibited from croaking.

In California, it is against the law to sell snakes street-side.

Research your State Statues reference books (located in most community or university libraries) to find out if your state has any strange herpetofauna laws or ordinances. Use index cards to record your findings and include the following information:

- Law/Ordinance Name/Number
- Description
- Year Passed
- Historical Information (if available)

Unusual Uses

In many countries, herpetofauna have been used, or are used, in unusual ways. Use the latitude-longitude coordinates on the Herpetofauna Map to locate the mystery countries.

1. In three countries, the Ornate Dabb lizard is used not only for food and leather goods, but also for medicine.

    25 N-45 E _____ **30 N-32 E** _____ **31 N-35 E** _____
    Country Country Country

2. In this country, the Ornate Dabb lizard is used as shark bait.   **32 N-6 W** _____
    Country

3. In this country the shell of the Red Toad-headed turtle is used as a musical instrument by some Tukanoan tribes.

    10 S-50 W _____
    Country

4. White Dragon salamanders are dried and used to provide relief for stomach troubles in this country. Centuries ago, in the same country, toad venom was used to stop gum-bleeding and to cure toothaches.

    30 N-110 E _____
    Country

5. The larva of the Axolotl is eaten as a delicacy in this country.

    25 N-100 W _____
    Country

6. Agriculturists released the Giant Marine toad in Texas and Hawaii to control beetles that were damaging the sugarcane crops. The plan was so successful that the toads were introduced in this country.

    30 S-140 E _____
    Country

7. In this country, Cobra is eaten deep-fried.

    16 N-101 E _____
    Country

8. Poisonous Sea snakes are eaten as a delicacy in this country.

    36 N-133 E _____
    Country

Herpetofauna Map

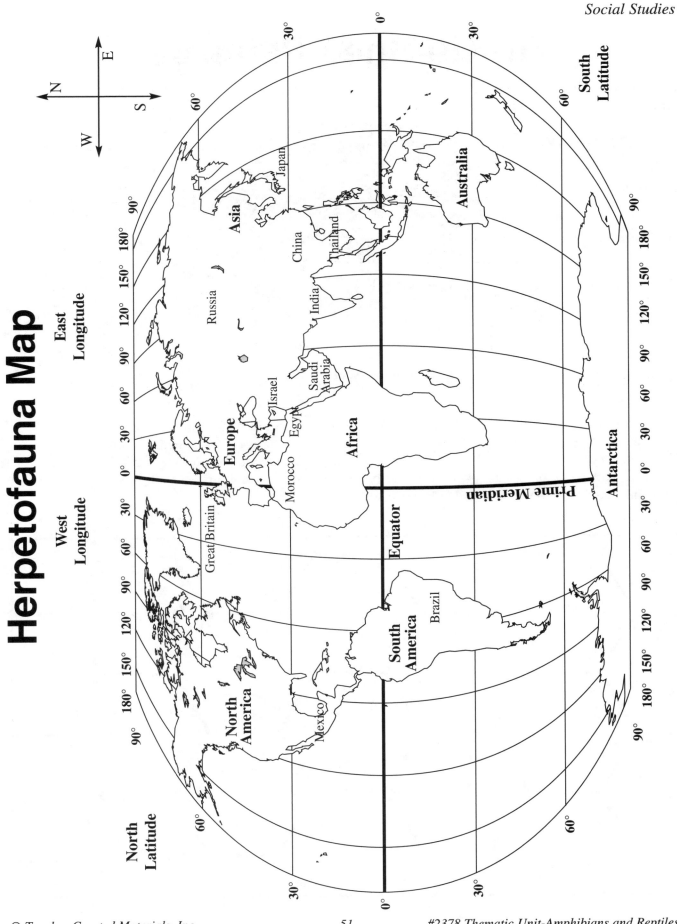

Turtle-Shell Patterns

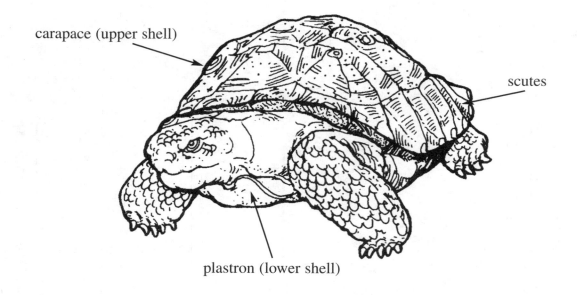

carapace (upper shell)

scutes

plastron (lower shell)

The American Box turtle has a hinged shell. When its head and legs are drawn in, its shell closes completely. Most Box turtles have semi-regular geometric patterns on their shells. Look at photographs or illustrations of Box-turtle shell patterns. Choose one and study it carefully. Create a repetitive pattern in the box below by repeatedly drawing your chosen turtle's shell pattern. Cut out your finished design on the side-edge lines; display.

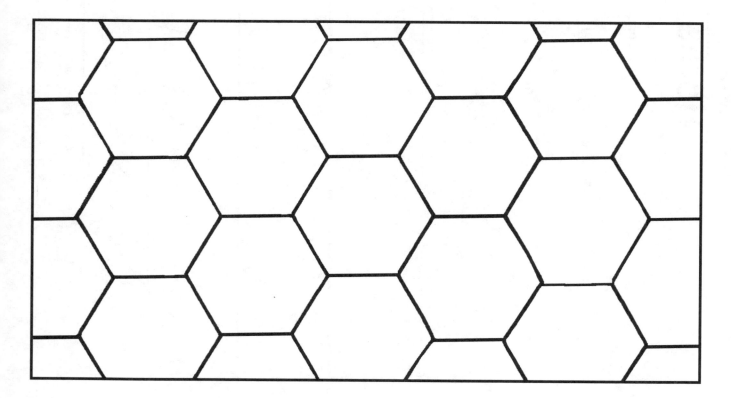

What is a Tuatara?

Tuatara reptiles live on some of the small islands off of the coast of New Zealand. Tuatara is a Maori word meaning "peaks along the back." Tuataras are among the coldest of the cold-blooded reptiles. If their body temperature rises to what is considered normal for most reptiles, Tuataras die. Tuataras can live to be 70–100 years old. It takes their eggs 12-15 months to hatch and they do not reach adulthood until 11–13 years of age. Tuataras became extinct on the mainland of New Zealand in the mid-19th century. This event caused them to become protected in 1895. In the 20th century, even though they have had endangerment protection, almost 14 of the 40 reported populations have disappeared. Today they are at a greater-than-ever risk of extinction.

Follow the directions below to mathematically depict a Tuatara.

Directions

1. Locate List A's coordinate points on the Tuatara Grid. Place a dot at the point of each intersection. (**Helpful Hints:** The coordinates are listed using Axis X–Axis Y. Check off the coordinates as you graph them on the grid and draw a connecting line between the dots as you progress. Do not wait until you are finished plotting the coordinates. It becomes too confusing.)

2. Follow the same procedure in Step 1 using Lists B, C, D, and E. If you have plotted the correct coordinate dots you will now see a Tuatara staring back at you!

List A			List B	List C	List D	List E
Start	24–13	24–8	**Start**	**Start**	**Start**	Place one
2–10	26–12	22–6	22–6	14–6	3–9	large dot
4–12	26–13	24–5	20–6	12–6	4–9	on 5–11.
6–13	28–12	22–3	18–6	10–7	6–9	
8–14	28–13	24–4	16–6	8–7	**Stop**	
10–13	30–12	22–2	16–7	6–8		
10–15	32–11	24–3	14–6	4–8		
12–15	34–10	24–2	14–5	2–10		
14–14	36–10	25–4	12–4	**Stop**		
14–15	38–10	26–3	14–4			
16–14	36–9	26–5	13–3			
16–15	34–8	24–6	14–3			
18–14	32–8	**Stop**	14–2			
18–15	30–7		16–4			
20–14	28–7		16–6			
22–13	26–7		**Stop**			
22–14	24–6					
24–12	26–8					

Tuatara Grid

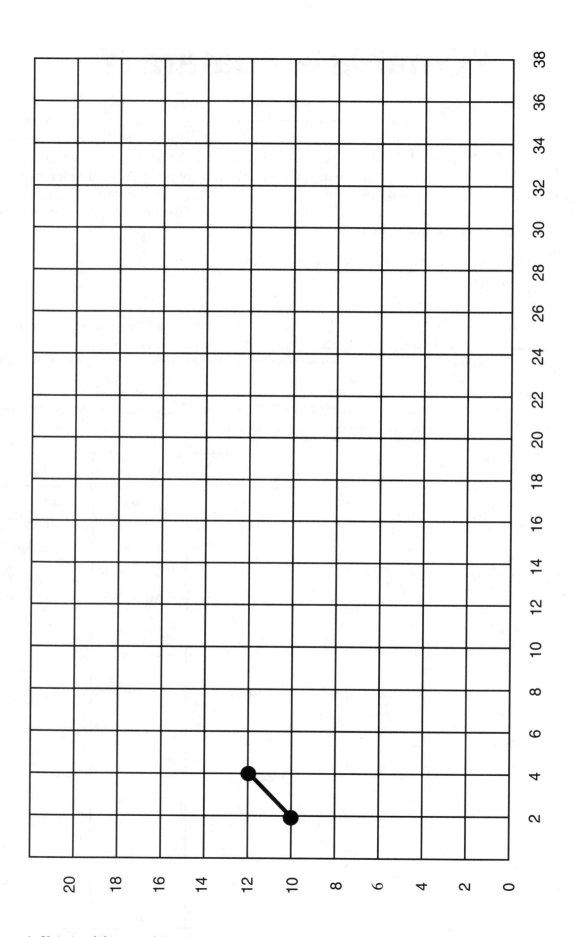

Species Populations

This chart displays the changes in Herpetofauna populations over a 22-year period. Complete the chart by recording the increases.

A pictograph uses pictures or symbols to represent information. The pictograph's key reflects the value for each picture or symbol. (See page 56.)

Create a Species-Populations Pictograph. Study the pictograph template and key. Determine how many frogs, caecilians, salamanders, and lizards you will need to cut out (below) to adequately represent the increases in species populations.

	Number of Species		Increase
	1975	1997	
Frogs	2000	3900	
Caecilians	70	163	
Salamanders and Newts	250	400	
Lizards	2500	3800	

(Note: If the number of an increased species is less than 100, use a proportional part of its symbol.) Glue your cut-out symbols onto the pictograph.

Frogs   **Caecilians**   **Salamanders**   **Lizards**

Species-Populations Pictograph

**Increases in Species Population
1975–1997**

Frogs	
Caecilians	
Salamanders	
Lizards	

Key

=100 =100 =100 =100

The Call of the Wild

Amphibian	Duration	Sound
Plains Spadefoot	1 second	hoarse trill
Cascades Frog	$\frac{1}{5}$ of a second	low-pitched
Canyon Treefrog	up to 3 seconds	nasal, same-tone notes
Plains Leopard Frog	$\frac{1}{3}$ of a second	guttural chuckle
Couch's Spadefoot	1 second	bleat of a lamb
Brinkley's Chorus Frog	1 second	raspy trill
Chorus Frog	2 seconds	rising note-scale trill

In the chart below, arrange the amphibians according to the length of their calls from the shortest to the longest. Don't forget the American toad!

Amphibian	Duration of Call

Don't croak, but the American toad's call lasts 20 seconds!

Call-Duration Bar Graph

Create a bar graph representing these amphibians' call durations.

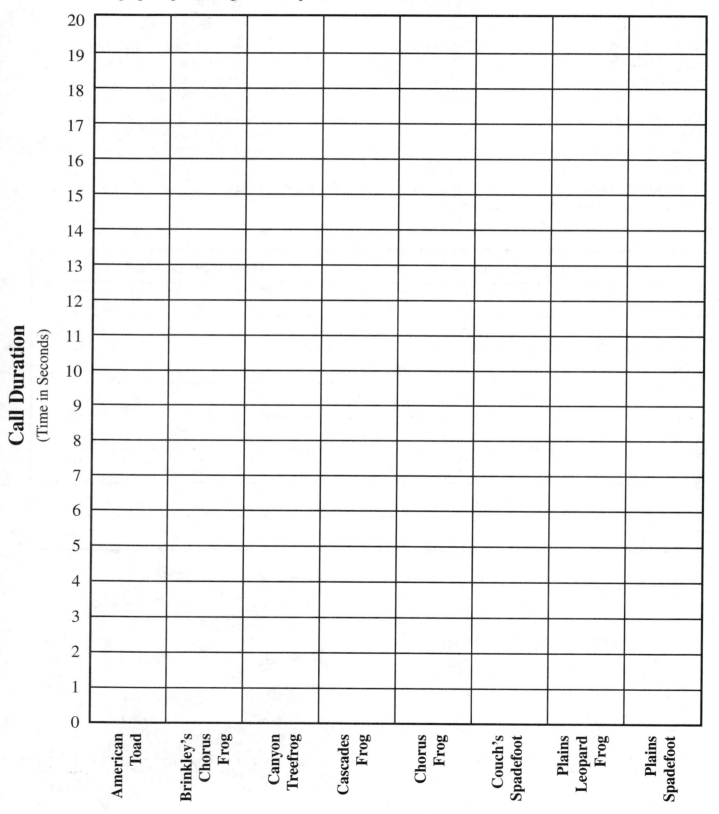

Herpetile Pets

Reptiles and amphibians are not considered domestic animals, even though they have been bred in captivity. Many people choose to keep reptiles as pets due to their ease of care. Many reptiles only have to be fed once a week. Some go without eating for a longer period of time. This makes it easy to go on a short vacation, as long as water is available for them. Be aware that unlike reptiles, amphibians quite often require a lot of care.

Another plus for herpetile pets is that they are quiet and do not require "affection." They also do not need the companionship that dogs or other animals often insist upon.

Caring for Herpetiles

- Learn everything you can about your prospective pet by reading, visiting pet stores, and talking to herpetile pet owners.

- Learn where to shop for your exotic pet. It is wiser and safer to acquire these pets from licensed pet stores rather than getting them "from the wild."

- Learn what type of habitat your desired pet enjoys and reproduce that environment to ensure good health and longevity. Are there any unusual requirements to consider?

- Learn what kind of food your new pet will need. Will that food be easy to obtain throughout the year?

- Learn your state's reptile-care requirements. Is it legal in your state for you to have the kind of animal you are planning on choosing? Does your state require the animal's owner to apply for an exotic-animal license?

Safety Precautions

The Bad News—Reptiles can harbor *Salmonella* bacteria.

The Good News—By following these safety precautions, you would be more likely to contract a *Salmonella* infection from uncooked meat than from handling reptiles:

1. After handling or cleaning your herpetile pet, always wash your hands immediately with a disinfectant soap.

2. If you have a cut or sore on your hands, handle your reptile while wearing gloves.

3. At all times, while handling your herpetile pet, keep your hands away from your mouth.

4. Always supervise herpetile-handling by anyone other than yourself, the herpetile's owner.

5. Be especially cautious with herpetiles around children under 5 years of age, as well as senior citizens. (Their immune systems are weaker.)

Designer Snakes

Owner-bred snakes, which display colors or patterns rarely seen in the wild, are called Designer snakes. A breeder is always looking to see if a snake has an unique design or color mutation and then breeds that snake in hopes that its offspring will likewise carry that mutant gene.

Why are snake breeders interested in refining the mutations? The more unusual the design or coloring, the higher the selling price can be to prospective pet owners.

In the mid-1980s, an extremely rare albino python was sold for $20,000. In economic terms, the *scarcity* (not many available) of an albino python and the *high demand* (many people wanting it) caused the price to soar. Today breeding has made the *supply* (availability) of non-patterned albino pythons so plentiful that the price has dropped to $150.

1. Based on the information above, explain how the relationship between supply and demand affects the price of a Designer snake.

_____

_____

_____

_____

2. The going rate for an ordinary Burmese python is $100, but a labyrinth-patterned, Albino Burmese python can cost up to $1,500. In economic terms, explain why the prices are so different.

_____

_____

_____

_____

3. Describe what would happen economically if breeders produce more albino pythons than pet owners want.

_____

_____

_____

_____

Special Snacks

In central Florida there is a store that specializes in alligator snacks.

Alligator Snacks	Weight	Single	Container	
Smoked Alligator Meat Stick	1 oz./28g	$2	Jar of 30 sticks	$39.95
Smoked Alligator Jerky Strip	.66 oz./21g	$2	Jar of 30 strips	$39.95
Smoked Gator Sausage	12 oz./350g chubb	$14.95	Box of 6 chubbs	$77.70
Smoked Gator Bites	2 oz./50g pkg.	$2.60	Box of 30 bites	$69.00
Smoked Gator Chew	5 oz./128g can	$2.49	12 can sleeve	$27.00
Smoked Alligator Gift Pack (4 meat sticks, 4 jerky strips, 1 chubb sausage, 1 can Gator Chew)				$29.95

1. Using the price list, how much would it cost to buy snacks for 12 people? (Each person needs to receive a one-ounce taste of each type of 'gator snack: stick, strip, sausage, bites, and chew.) Make a chart on the back of this paper listing your order. Include a column for each item, the amount needed, and the price. Be sure to tally up and record the total cost of your order.

2. Instead of buying items separately, how much money do you save by purchasing one gift pack? (Show your work on the back of this paper.)

3. As a consumer, decide which snack gives you the most product in one jar—the jerky strips or the meat sticks. Give one possible reason for the difference in price. _____

_____

4. Which is the better buy:

   A. 12 single cans of Gator Chew or one sleeve? _____Why? _____

   _____

   B. Six 12 oz./35g chubbs of Gator Sausage or one box of 6 chubbs? _____

   Why?_____

   _____

   C. One box of Gator Bites or thirty 2 oz./50g packages?_____

   Why?_____

   _____

Gharial Designs

Gharials, or Gavials, are huge, fish-eating crocodilians. They have extremely slender and long snouts, unlike a crocodile, whose snout is broad and flat.

Gharial **Crocodile**

Materials

- one Single Design stencil (page 63), reproduced onto tagboard and cut out
- one 4¹/₂" x 12" (23 cm x 30 cm) sheet of green construction paper
- one 9" x 12" (23 cm x 30 cm) sheet of white construction paper
- scissors
- pencil
- glue

Directions

1. Place the green sheet of construction paper in a vertical position.

2. Position the cut-out stencil so that the flat edge of the stencil meets with the far-right edge of the sheet of paper. Trace around the stencil with the pencil; remove stencil.

12" (30 cm)

3. Cut out the Gharial shape along the traced pencil line.
   (**Note:** Do not discard the cut-away portion.)

4. Fold the white sheet of construction paper in half lengthwise; crease the center line; re-open and lay flat on desk or tabletop. Place the cut-out green Gharial half on top of the white sheet, matching up the flat edge of the Gharial to the white sheet's center line; glue into place.

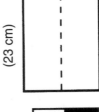

9" (23 cm)

5. Using the cut-away green Gharial section, flip it over and match the flat-side edge to the right-side edge of the white paper; glue into place.

Optional: For a double Gharial design, follow the illustrated directions.

12" (30 cm)   6" (15 cm)

9"   9"
(23 cm)   (23 cm)

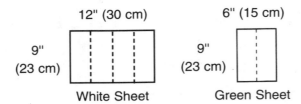   

White Sheet   Green Sheet

Place the white sheet horizontally on a flat surface. Fold the white sheet in half, then in half again; crease and unfold. (You will have four sections.) Follow the basic steps above using the double Gharial design (page 63) to create a double design.

Gharial Stencils

Single Design   **Double Design**

Pigmentation Color Wheel

Materials

- white construction paper
- red, yellow, and blue tempera paints
- small mixing bowl
- paintbrush
- water
- black marking pen

Directions

1. Using the color wheel below as a guideline, paint the three primary colors (circles) on a white construction paper palate. (**Note:** Clean your brush thoroughly after each color.)

2. In the small bowl, mix an equal amount of these primary colors: red and yellow. Paint the (square) area in between the red and yellow circles with the secondary color created; thoroughly clean the brush and the bowl.

3. In the small bowl, mix an equal amount of these primary colors: red and blue. Paint the (square) area in between the red and blue circles with the secondary color created; thoroughly clean the brush and the bowl.

4. Again, in the small bowl, mix an equal amount of these primary colors: blue and yellow. Paint the remaining (square) area with the secondary color created; thoroughly clean the brush and the bowl.

5. Using the marking pen, label the primary and discovered secondary colors.

Answer the following questions by observing the completed color wheel.

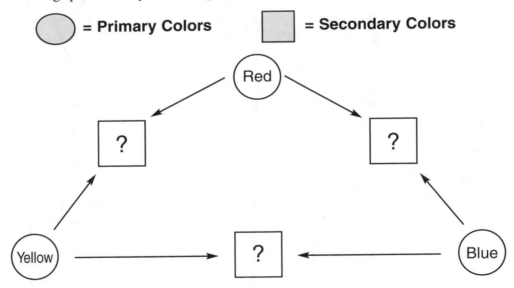

1. Some green frogs are lacking a yellow pigmentation. What colors would these frogs be?

_____

2. The Red-eared Slider turtles have been photographed with pigment defects in which the turtles are yellow instead of their usual green color. Which color pigment were these turtles missing?

_____

Gecko Links

Geckos have short legs, wide claws, and rounded toe pads. On the bottom of each toe pad there are scales covered with hair-like bristles. Each bristle's tip has a tiny suction cup that allows a gecko to walk up walls and on ceilings.

Follow the directions below to create linking geckos that you can use to tape onto the walls or ceiling of your own room or the classroom.

Materials

- Gecko Pattern (below), reproduced onto tagboard and cut out
- scissors
- adding-machine paper
- pencil
- transparent tape
- crayons or markers

Directions

1. Starting at either end, fold over a five-inch (13 cm) section of the adding-machine tape; crease the fold. Using an accordion-fold pattern, continue folding the paper until you have seven folded sections, crease the folds.

2. Place the cut-out gecko pattern on top of the folded adding-machine paper. Trace the outline shape onto the paper with the pencil; remove pattern and cut along pencil lines. (**Note:** Do not cut the folded ends of the paper near the gecko's nose and tail tip!) Discard the cut-away paper; open up the gecko links. If desired, color the geckos.

3. Repeat Steps 1 and 2 to create as many gecko links as desired. Tape the ends of the links together to create one continuous pattern.

Gecko Pattern

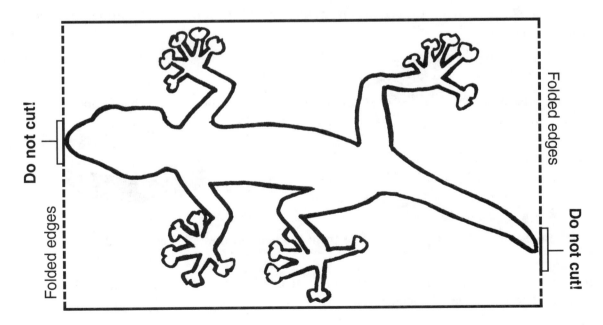

Snake Tricks

Here are some snake tricks that are designed to trick the eye.

Materials

- construction paper
- scissors
- marking pen
- transparent tape

Basic Directions

1. Make three 2" x 24" (5 cm x 61 cm) construction-paper strips.

2. Round off the ends of each strip. Add snake eyes to one end of each of the three strips.

Snake Trick 1

1. On one snake strip, draw a line from its head to its tail that is 1" (2.54 cm) from the left side-edge of the snake.

2. Bring the tail around in a circle-fashion until it meets the snake's head. Half-twist the tail and tape its tail to the snake's head.

3. Using the scissors, cut along the marked line until you have cut the snake in two. What happens to the snake?

Snake Trick 2

1. On a second snake strip, draw two lines from the head to the tail ⁵⁄₈"(1.67 cm) from the left- and right-side edges.

2. Bring the tail around in a circle-fashion until it meets the snake's head. Full-twist the tail (in other words, two half-twists) and tape it to the snake's head.

3. Using the scissors, cut one of the drawn lines; then cut the other line. What happens to the snake this time?

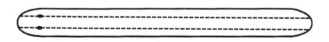

Snake Trick 3

1. On the remaining snake strip, draw a line from the head to the tail that is 1" (2.54 cm) from the left side.

2. Bring the tail around in a circle-fashion until it meets the snake's head. Make a full-twist with the tail and tape it to the snake's head.

3. Cut on the line. What is the result this time?

Herpetology Events

Here are some activities that will help you in the assessment process of your Amphibians and Reptiles unit.

I'm a Herpetologist! Game

To play, form two to four teams. While playing the game, encourage the students to verbally share their responses. This will allow you to assess the level of general mastery. (**Note:** This game can also be played by two to four individuals and would make a nice addition to a learning center area.)

Preparation

1. Reproduce the game cards (page 68) onto tagboard. Cut out the cards; laminate for durability, if desired.

2. Reproduce the game board (pages 69–70). Trim along the outer edges, match up the two center-line edges; glue the game-board pieces onto an 18" x 26" (46 cm x 66 cm) piece of tagboard and trim the edges. If desired, color and laminate for durability.

3. Display the game board. Place the game cards (mixed up and face down) onto the game board, matching the cards to the game board's corresponding placement symbols.

4. Provide a marker for each team or individual players.

Directions

1. The first team, or individual player, draws and reads a card from the star-card pile and moves accordingly until reaching an Animal circle. The three remaining teams, or players, likewise choose a star card and move accordingly. (**Note:** The Star card not only indicates which path to take, but also indicates the taking-turns order. Therefore, the first team (player) to choose a star card may not be the first one to go when it is time to choose from the circle-card pile.)

2. Draw a circle card. If a characteristic is correctly identified, the team or player proceeds along the maze path to the Status rectangle. If not correctly identified, the team or player must wait and try again during the next round of turns. (**Note:** The game cards are always returned to the bottom of their respective decks.)

3. Draw a rectangle card. Answer the endangerment question posed based on the animal and its characteristic correctly identified during the team's or player's last turn. If the information shared is correct, slide the marker to the Question-mark oval; if incorrect, wait until the next turn to pick a rectangle card and try again.

4. Draw an oval card. When the mystery question is correctly answered, the team's or player's marker is moved to the Herpetologist portion of the game board and the honorary title of Herpetologist is awarded (page 76).

Multimedia Presentations

Using available software, such as Hyperstudio® or Powerpoint®, encourage your students to work in small groups or individually to create a slide show presentation.

Herpetologist Game Cards

★ Go through Maze 1.	★ Go through Maze 2.	★ Go through Maze 3.	★ Go through Maze 4.
● Name a unique Tree Frog characteristic.	● Name a unique Crocodile characteristic.	● Name a unique Gecko characteristic.	● Name a unique Boa Constrictor characteristic.
■ Is your animal's endangerment status stable?	■ Is your animal's endangerment status rare?	■ Is your animal's endangerment status extinct?	■ Is your animal's endangerment status vulnerable?
● What is one geographic location where your animal lives?	● What habitat does your animal prefer?	● What are three foods your animal likes to eat?	● Who are your animal's natural enemies?

● Name a unique Salamander characteristic.	● Name a unique Caecilian characteristic.		
● Name a unique Tuatara characteristic.	● Name a unique Sea Turtle characteristic.		
■ Is your animal's endangerment status threatened?	■ Is your animal's endangerment status endangered?		
● Is your animal a reptile or an amphibian?	● How does your animal defend itself?		

Herpetologist Game Board

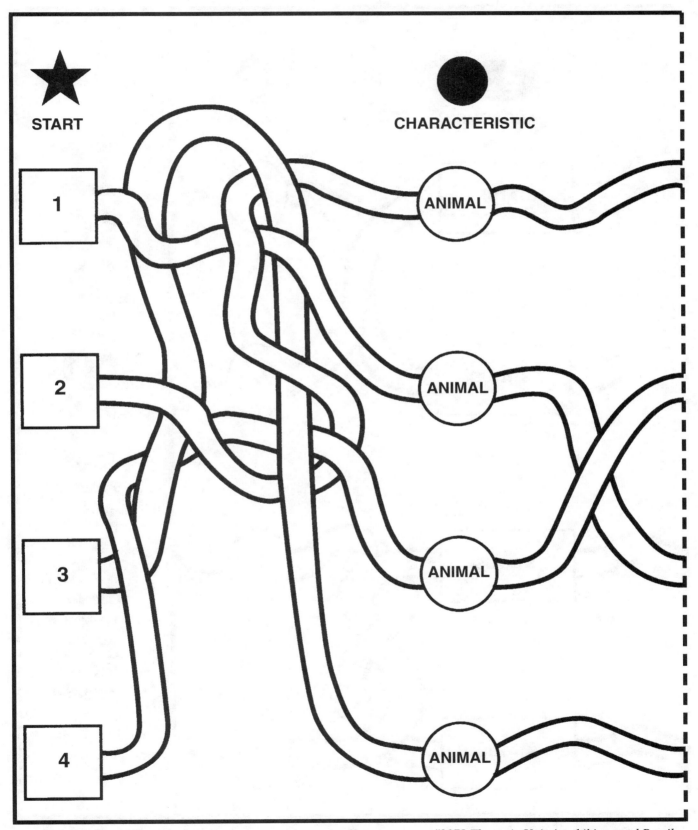

START

CHARACTERISTIC

1

2

3

4

ANIMAL

ANIMAL

ANIMAL

ANIMAL

Herpetologist Game Board *(cont.)*

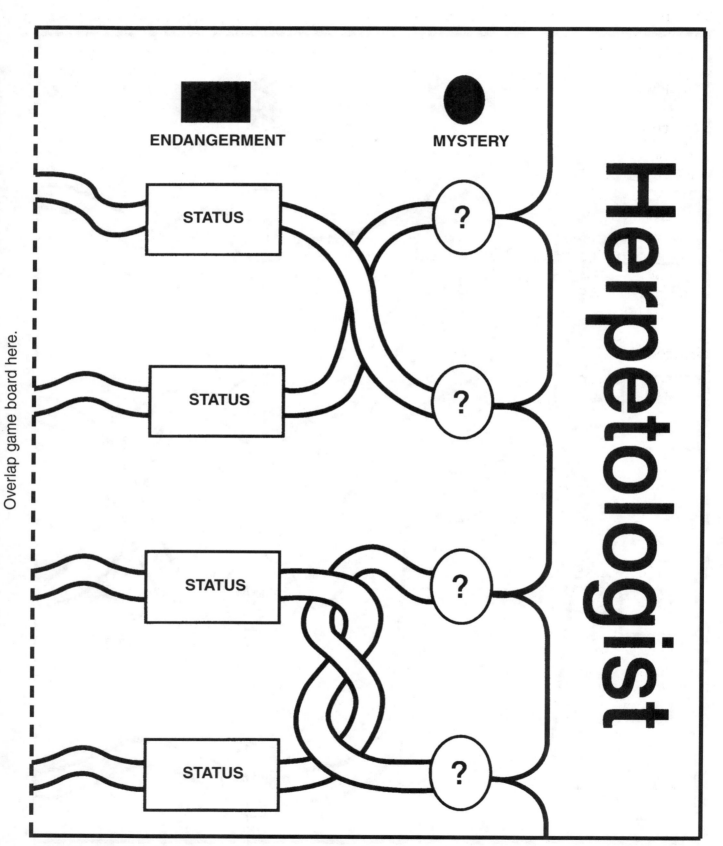

ENDANGERMENT

MYSTERY

STATUS

STATUS

STATUS

STATUS

?

?

?

?

Overlap game board here.

Herpetologist

Turtle Simulation

The turtle is the only reptile that has a shell. It has the ability to pull its head and legs into its shell for protection from predators. There are approximately 250 different species of turtles worldwide and more that 40 of those species are listed as endangered. In order for their continued survival, turtle conservation is essential. By participating in this turtle simulation, your students will realize just how difficult it is for turtles to survive.

Materials

- several lengths of rope (enough to mark-off the playing field)
- approximately 1500 dried (uncooked) Navy beans
- plastic, self-sealing, sandwich-size bags (one per turtle)
- 2 packages of 3" x 5" (8 cm x 13 cm) index cards
- wearable signs (cardboard and string work well) that identify limiting factors: Predator, Hunters, Pollution, Habitat Loss, Food Shortage.
- area identification signs (cardboard, tent-style signs work well): Year Area, Year Area, Nest Area, Beach Area, Open Sea, Sea Grass, Sea Grass
- empty bucket (fatality area)

Directions

1. Using the rope, set up the playing field as shown. (**Note:** The game area can be made as small or as large as you'd like.)

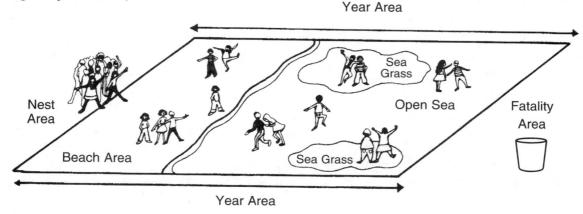

2. Divide your class into two teams. Half of the students will role-play hatching turtles. Each hatching-turtle student represents 100 turtles, therefore give each student 100 Navy beans in a sealed, plastic bag. Have the hatching-turtles students stand in the Nest Area.

3. The remaining students will represent the Limiting Factors by wearing the prepared signs: Predator, Hunters, Pollution, Habitat Loss, and Food Shortage. (**Note:** Try to have half of the limiting factors be land-based, the other half sea-based.)

4. Explain to your students that this simulation is to demonstrate the hardships in the life cycle of sea turtles.

Turtle Simulation *(cont.)*

Directions *(cont.)*

5. Explain the playing field:

   Nest Area—the area where the turtle eggs are laid and hatched. When the turtles are ten years old, they return, and once again, begin the egg-laying life cycle.

   Beach Area—the area over which the baby turtles must cross to get into the open sea. This is often where newly born sea turtles lose their lives.

   Year Areas—these areas are where the turtle-representing students need to go to get Growth Cards (index cards). They can only receive one Growth Card at a time. Also, they must travel in a back-and-forth pattern between the two Year Areas to receive their needed 10 Growth Cards (each card represents one year of growth). **Important Note:** Once a student has received 10 Year Cards, he or she needs to go back to the Nest Area to lay new eggs. When the student arrives in the Nest Area, he or she deserves a two-minute rest break. That student then receives an additional 100 Navy beans (baby turtles) and sets out once again to try and cross the Beach Area back into the Open Sea.

   Open Sea Area—this is where the turtles live and roam for ten years until they have reached maturity and return to the nesting area.

   Sea Grass Areas—these are the areas where turtles—four years and younger (students holding 0–4 Growth Cards)—can hide from predators for up to one minute.

   Fatality Area—this is where the destroyed (tagged) turtles are laid to rest. If tagged, the turtle-representing student must give the limiting-factor student a pre-determined number of turtles (Navy beans):

   - Tagged in Beach Area = 20 turtles
   - Tagged in Open Sea Area (4 years or younger) = 10 turtles
   - Tagged in Open Sea Area (5 years or older) = 2 turtles

6. Explain the game's rules:

   - The turtles must survive the ever-present Limiting Factors. They are to try and pass by the Limiting Factors without being tagged. (**Note:** The students wearing the limiting-factor signs must stay within their pre-designated area. For example, a Beach-Area limiting factor student cannot enter the Open-Sea Area.)

   - Limiting-factor students may not tag the same turtle-representing student twice in a row. After tagging four turtle-representing students, the limiting-factor student must deposit his or her collected destroyed turtles (Navy beans) into the Fatality Area (bucket). (**Note:** This student may not tag any turtles on his or her way to the Fatality Area.)

   - Turtle-representing students that lose all 100 turtles (Navy beans) must go and sit by the Fatality bucket.

7. Explain the game's goal: The turtle-representing students' eggs are "hatched;" they then attempt to cross the beach area to go into the open sea, live there safely for ten years, then return to their nesting area to reproduce.

After the simulation experience has been conducted, take time to allow your students to summarize and share the feelings they experienced during the game. If possible, invite another class to play. Allow your students to be the facilitators and after-simulation discussion leaders.

Bulletin-Board Ideas

A Reading Metamorphosis

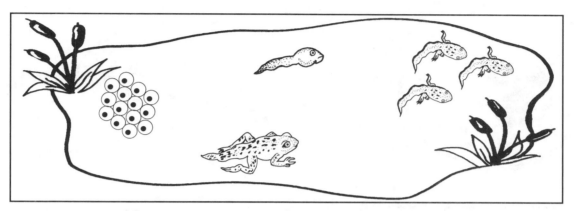

Prepare your display board by first covering the entire background with yellow bulletin-board paper. Next, create a large, free-form pond from blue bulletin-board paper; attach to board. Add small patches of cattails (brown and green bulletin-board paper). Reproduce the egg pattern (page 74), one per student. Cut out the eggs and add a student's name to each egg; form an egg mass (cluster of eggs) near the left edge of the pond. (**Note:** It is recommended that you also reproduce and cut out as many Tadpole 1s, Tadpole 2s, Froglets, Frogs, and Lily Pads [page 75] as you will need.)

When a student completes the reading of a pre-determined book, metamorphosis begins! He or she exchanges his or her egg (removing it from board) for a Tadpole 1. The student colors the tadpole and adds it to the top area of the pond. After reading a second book, the student exchanges his or her Tadpole 1 (removing it from board) for a Tadpole 2 colors it and adds it to the right-side area of the pond. After the next read book is read, the student's Tadpole 2 is replaced with a colored Froglet that is added near the bottom edge of the pond. After the fifth book has been read, the student exchanges the Froglet for a Frog and Lily Pad. The student fills in the Lily Pad, colors the Frog, and places both on the bulletin board in the center of the pond.

(Note: The metamorphosis exchange process can also be used as a behavioral reward system wherein the students earn a pre-determined number of points for each "change." A special prize is awarded for reaching the Frog level, such as an extra recess or a no-homework night or week.

Weird Science

Create a bulletin board wherein the students gather or create their own illustrations of weird (unusual-looking) amphibians and reptiles. Next to the displayed creatures, list their names and where they are geographically located.

Bulletin-Board Patterns

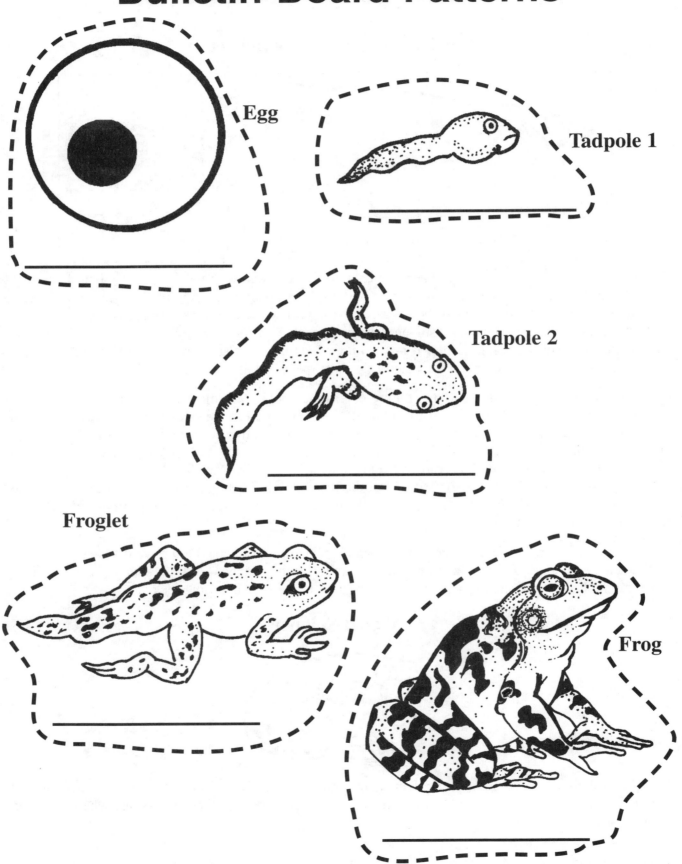

Egg

Tadpole 1

Tadpole 2

Froglet

Frog

74

Ask an Expert

Guide your students towards generating a list of questions they would like answered. Create a reference display of their questions. Be certain to include a list of herpetofauna addresses and Web sites that may be contacted to answer the posed questions. When a student has received a written response, have him or her share it with the class and then post it on the display board.

Herp Clubs and Organizations

American Federation of Herpetoculturists
Box 300067
Escondido, CA 92030

California Turtle & Tortoise Club
Westchester Chapter
Box 90252
Los Angeles, CA 90009

Central Florida Herpetological Society
P.O. Box 3277
Winter Haven, Florida 33885

New York Turtle and Tortoise Society
163 Amsterdam Avenue, Suite 365
New York, New York 10023

Reptiles, Inc.
29820 High Street
Centralia, IL 62801

Publications

The Bridge
(A quarterly newsletter concerning turtles and tortoises.)
160 North Fairview Avenue
Goleta, GA 95117

Captive Breeding Magazine
Snake Bite, Inc.
Box 87100
Canton, MI 48187

Herpetological Review
16333 Deer Path Lane
Clovis, California 93612

Informational Services

Ask the Vet
P.O. Box 780073
San Antonio, Texas 78278-0073

World Conservation Monitoring Center
ATTN: Information Officer
219 Huntington Road
Cambridge, United Kingdom CB3 0DL

Web Sites

Chicago's Lincoln Park Zoo: The Reptiles
www.lpzoo.com/animals/herps/herpslist.html
You will find a variety of species data sheets as well as definitions for both amphibians and reptiles.

Marine Turtles
www.turtles.org
A wonderful site filled with detailed information on a variety of marine turtles.

Reptiles and Amphibians
www.webcom.com/~iwcwww/wurld_wild_web/reptiles.html
This site has a plethora of web connections on specific species as well as general herpetofauna resources.

Reptile Mall
www.reptilemall.com/care.html
This site has pet-care sheets for over 50 different amphibians and reptiles.

Turtles, Sea Turtles, and Tortoises-On the Web
www.xmission.com/~gastown/herpmed/chelonia.htm
A great site for links to a vast array of information and resources.

Bibliography

Bill Wallace Literature

(Note: Mr. Wallace has written many more titles than those listed. Check your school or public library, or conduct an on-line book search to locate his complete inventory of titles.)

The Backward Dog. Minstrel, 1997.
A Dog Called Kitty. Holiday House, 1998.
The Flying Flea, Callie, and Me. Minstrel, 1999.
Red Dog. Pocket Books, 1994.
Watchdog and the Coyotes. Minstrel, 1995.

Herpetofauna Fiction

Calmenson, Stephen. *Rockin' Reptiles*. Demco, 1998.
Chang, Heidi. *Elaine and the Flying Frog*. Random House, 1991.
Clifford, Eth. *Harvey's Horrible Snake Disaster*. Pocket Books, 1986.
Conford, Ellen. *The Frog Princess of Pelham*. Little Brown, 1997.
Coville, Bruce. *Jennifer Murdley's Toad*. Pocket Books, 1993.
Dahl, Roald. *The Enormous Crocodile*. Puffin, 1993.
Krailing, Tessa. *Snake Alarm*. Hippo, 1998.
Mazer, Anne. *The Salamander Room*. Knopf, 1997.
McMurtry, Ken. *Beware the Snake's Venom*. Bantam, 1995.
Phillips, Louis. *Alligator Wrestling and You*. Avon, 1992.
Sherman, Gisele Tobien. *There's a Snake in the Toilet*. Pocket Books, 1995.
Stuart, Jesse. *Old Ben*. Jesse Stuart Foundation, 1991.
Woodruff, Elvira. *The Secret Funeral of Slim Jim the Snake*. Holiday House, 1993.

Herpetofauna Nonfiction

Amphibians. Eyewitness Books, 1991.
Chatfield, June. *A Look Inside Reptiles*. Reader's Digest, 1995.
Conant, Roger. Robert Stebbins, and Joseph Collins. *Peterson First Guides Reptiles and Amphibians*. Houghton Mifflin, 1992.
Gunzi, Christy. *Amphibians and Reptiles*. Advan Marketing, 1998.
Parker, Nancy. *Frogs, Toads, Lizards, and Salamanders*. William Morrow, 1996.
Reptiles. Eyewitness Books, 1991.
Ruiz, Andres. *Reptiles and Amphibians: Birth & Growth*. Sterling, 1996.
Ruiz, Jim. *The Giant Book of Snakes and Slithery Creatures*. Copper Beech, 1998.
The Snake Book. Dorling Kindersley, 1997.

CD-ROMs

Amphibians and Reptiles. Junior Nature Guides Series. ICE Integrated Communications & Entertainment, 489 Queen St. E. Toronto, Ontario, Canada.
Eyewitness Encyclopedia of Nature. Software. Dorling Kindersley. 95 Madison Avenue, New York, N.Y. 10016. 1-800-DKMM-575.

Videos

Cool Creature: Reptiles. Cochran Communications, 1994. 22 minutes.
Crocodiles: Here Be Dragons. National Geographic Video, 1900. 60 minutes.
Really Wild Animals: Dinosaurs and other Creatures Features. National Geographic Video, 1995, 47 minutes.

Answer Key

Page 8 Who Am I?

1. Sally
2. Tina
3. Ted
4. Jo Donna
5. Liz
6. Shane

Page 9 Cause and Effect

1. M	8. D
2. L	9. K
3. F	10. E
4. H	11. I
5. B	12. J
6. C	13. G
7. A	

Page 11 Liz and Lizard Probability

1. 9/15 or 3/5
2. 3/15 or 1/5
3. 1/15
4. 13/15 (87%)
5. 60%; 20%; 7%
6. skink; there is only one on the porch
7. chameleon; there are nine chameleons on the porch

Page 12 Turtle Trails

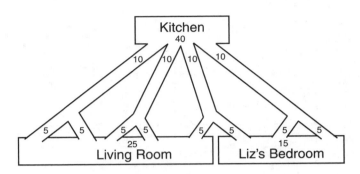

Living Room <u>25</u>
Liz's Bedroom <u>15</u>
Explanations will vary.

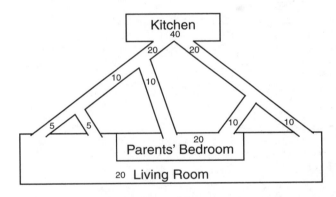

Living Room <u>20</u>
Parent's Bedroom <u>20</u>
Explanations will vary.

Page 26 Stick Out Your Tongue

1. Terrestrial Lizard
2. Glass Lizard
3. Iguana
4. Worm Lizard
5. Monitor Lizard
6. Gecko
7. Skink

Page 41 Amphibious Genetics

1. striped
2. mottled
3. 3
4. SS or Ss
5. ss
6. If the dominant gene is present, the frog is striped. If both the genes are recessive, it is mottled.

Page 47 Endangerment Chart

Endangerment Chart

Herpetofauna Name	Location	Endangerment Status	Reason for Status	Suggested Actions
Kemp's Ridley Turtle	Atlantic Ocean	Endangered	1) Deaths from nets 2) Egg loss	
Florida Gopher Tortoise	Southeastern United States	Vulnerable	Destruction of habitat from business growth and fires	
Axolotl	Mexico	Rare	In the future the number could be affected by the introduction of the non-native fish	Accept any reasonable answer.
Vegas Valley Leopard Frog	Las Vegas, Nevada	May already be extinct	Destruction of habitat	
St. Croix Ground Lizard	St. Croix, Virgin Island	Endangered	Restricted habitat	
California Black Legless Lizard	California	Endangered	Loss of habitat	
Eastern Indigo Snake	Georgia, South Carolina, Alabama, Florida	Vulnerable	In great demand for sale	

Page 50 Unusual Uses

1. Saudi Arabia: Egypt; Israel
2. Morocco
3. Brazil
4. China
5. Mexico
6. Australia
7. Thailand
8. Japan

Page 61 Special Snacks

1. Approximately $71.
2. $3.49
3. meat sticks (30 oz. instead of 19.80 oz. for strips)
4. A. sleeve (12 single cans cost $29.88)
   B. box (6 chubbs cost $89.70)
   C. box (30 packages cost $78)

Page 64 Pigmentation Color Wheel

1. blue
2. blue

Page 56 Species - Populations Pictograph

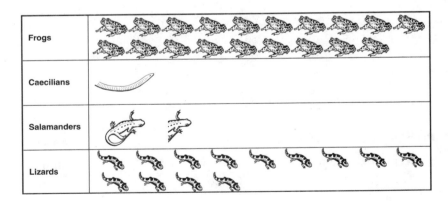